Northern Reaction

BILL MARCHANT

Cover art by Rose Marchant

Cover design by Howard Poole

ISBN: 1539068854
ISBN-13: 978-1539068853

DEDICATION

This book is dedicated to Mark Steyn, for first showing me the contradictions on which modernity is built

Contents

FOREWORD

Gay marriage is now a conservative value. "Because it's 2015" is an acceptable justification for policy. Multiculturalism is our national identity (which is to say we don't **HAVE** a national identity). Saying the wrong thing about the wrong protected class will get you hauled in front of an Orwellianly named Human Rights Tribunal. Conservative media is almost nonexistent. Eight years of a Conservative government resulted in no significant rightward developments. Ford Nation went up in a puff of crack smoke. The federal government is currently headed by a Social Justice prettyboy from a family that deserves Damnatio Memoriae.

In short, Canada is a wasteland for Rightists. If America Is A Communist Country, as Mencius Moldbug famously declared, that goes double for Canada. We're the place where every little piece of social engineering is test-marketed before the big product rollout Stateside. It's bleak but not hopeless for Canadian Rightists. If you're reading this then chances are that you know of the Alt-Right, that motley coalition of Right-wing rebels united in their opposition to mainstream conservatism. Operating mostly online, they have in a short period of time exposed America's Conservative Movement as little more than a token opposition to Liberalism and begun to impact national discourse. Can this successfully be replicated north of the 49th Parallel? I would say yes. However there are obstacles. In America the Alt-Right has had a particular candidate that it rallied behind and who in turn created space for them to enter national politics. We in Canada should harbour no illusions about trying to take over our sorry excuse for a Conservative Party. All of the confirmed and rumoured candidates for the Cuckservative Party leadership race are useless to us. Trying to infiltrate the Party from the grassroots is a remote possibility. Doubtlessly, anyone espousing Alt-Right rhetoric of any kind can expect to be purged quickly. The Alt-Right in America was in a similar situation until a certain billionaire entered their Presidential race, so the idea can’t be discounted entirely. It isn't something I would bet on. If our electoral system changes then starting a Nationalist Party could work. It’s also something I wouldn't bet on. What can we do then? The answer is to begin attacking Canadian conservatism from the right by using the signature alt-right mix of serious writing and outright trolling. The goal should be to discredit Canada's conservatives and unmask them as mere liberals at half-speed. This worked wonders in the U.S and it should be even easier to do here because of how weak our conservatives are. Then build platforms such as Alt-Right websites with a distinctly Canadian viewpoint, start organizations in real life, and be ready to replace Canadian conservatism when it succumbs to the simultaneous pressure from Left and Right. I would like to go into further detail, but alas this is not the place.

One fresh voice doing his part to add homegrown perspectives to the Alt-Right is the author of this collection. From the informative ("Blame Canada For..") and insightful ("Don't Punch Right") to the humorous ("Taking Rap Lyrics Too Seriously") and the just plain weird ("Meme Magic, Trump, and Grant Morrison") these essays exemplify the things that Alt-Right commentary does best. If a few more people like Bill Marchant step up and start producing good content then maybe we can make the Great White North great again after all.

E. F. Silk

INTRODUCTION

Canada does not have anything approaching a viable nationalist movement. Or anything approaching America's Alt-Right.[1] Or the European Nouveau Droit.[2]

We have a far-left party in the NDP, a centre-left party in the Liberals, and a centre-right party in the Conservatives. There used to be a few farther-right options, but even they barely left the territory of centre-right, and they were pulled to the left when they merged into the Conservatives.

I think a big part of the lack of a far-right (or even just fully right) party in Canadian politics is a lack of anyone talking about that position and how the intellectual frameworks of the right elsewhere can be applied to the Canadian situation. We have people like Mark Steyn[3] repres enting a solidly right position, but despite the fact that he would be considered mainstream in America, in Canada he is seen by many as extreme. Mark Steyn can only be seen as extreme when there is nothing further right to compare him to. Free Northerner[4] is further right, but he blogs *from* Canada, and says little *about* Canada.

With all of that in mind, the purpose of Northern Reaction is to try to shift the Overton Window[5] in Canada just a bit further right.

There are two driving ideas behind this blog (besides the usual stuff) that will inform some of the content here.

The first is Hanlon's Razor: "Never attribute to malice that which is adequately explained by stupidity." This idea is just about the only thing that keeps me sane on a day to day basis. If I was to assume that every harmful or awful thing that politicians and academics do was done through malice, I would not be able to get anything done. By assuming stupidity, I can trust in the idea that if these people knew what they were doing wrong, they would not be doing it. That lets me keep going and hoping that, one day, minds could be changed.

The other idea is a quote from The Simpsons: "I may not know art, but I know what I hate." I don't have a comprehensive theory of government. I don't know whether democracy is good generally, could be good in theory, or will never be good. I don't know how much of IQ difference is genetic. But I know I communism is not the solution to government. I know that democracy is not always good. And I know that genetics account for something in IQ difference. So if some days this blog seems more Alt-Right, and on others more Neoreactionary or libertarian, it is because I'm not really advocating for a particular position, but rather against the things I hate.

So join me in my exploration of history, culture, politics and literature, all from a Canadian perspective.

---

[1] Essentially a right-wing populist movement. There are many factions within the group, so any single definition would be inadequate.

[2] A right-wing intellectual movement originating in France. I would strongly recommend reading some of the authors associated with this movement, particularly Alain de Benoist.

[3] Once a writer for Maclean's, and the man responsible for my first cold breath of reality after years of indoctrination, sadly he is now a persona-non-grata in Canada, and lives in New Hampshire.

[4] An excellent Canadian blogger. You can find his site at freenortherner.com

[5] The extent of discourse allowed in a given society or social situation, basically.

A QUICK NOTE ON SOURCES

I read a lot, and I read quickly. Mostly that's a good thing, but it means it's sometimes difficult to figure out where I read something on the fly. I will try my best to source the things I say here. However, I may occasionally believe that something doesn't need a source because it's common knowledge, when in fact it was only ever said once in a book I read from the 1700s. If that happens, and you find yourself thinking "That can't possibly be true", let me know. I will find that source.

Somehow.

Even though truth is not a defence in Canada (that fact will be the subject of a later post), I will strive to ensure that everything said on this blog is true.

BLAME CANADA FOR... PART 1: AFRICA

Or, why Canada is responsible for a surprising amount of what's wrong with the world today

Most people, if they think about Canada at all, think of hockey, poutine, snow, and maybe lumberjacks...

Chances are, you don't think of Canada's impact on world politics and culture. You probably think Canada has no impact on the world. I'm here to tell you that you're wrong. Canada has had an impact on the world. And that impact is not exactly all good.

This will be the first part in a series about how a shocking number of the problems going on in the world today can be traced back to Canada. So let's get right to it.

Canada is responsible for the fall of Rhodesia, and by extension, the end of successful Africa.

If you don't know about Rhodesia, you may think that "successful Africa" is an oxymoron. It's not. Rhodesia was a British colony, then briefly an independent nation, in the land that is now occupied by Zimbabwe. No, Rhodesia did not "become" Zimbabwe, any more than the serial killer that's sitting in your mom's place at the dinner table "has become" your mom. They both just happen to be in the same place as the previous thing.

COME GIVE MOMMY A KISS

Rhodesia was by all important factors a success. It had a high GDP, high median income, high standard of living. It was known as "The Breadbasket of Africa." The people in the colony, both black and white, had relatively high levels of freedom.

The "problem" with Rhodesia was that it was ruled by white Africans. The white minority ran the country, and while the black majority did have some minor influence on policy, it really was nothing compared to power the whites had. Essentially, Rhodesia took away black political freedom, in exchange for black personal freedom.[6] Whether this was "racist" or not does not matter. It worked.

This lasted until Rhodesia attempted to gain independence from Britain, as Ghana, Malawi, and Zambia had shortly before. The Queen was against giving Rhodesia independence, but the Prime Minister of Britain at the time, Harold Wilson, was not fundamentally opposed to granting Rhodesia independence. If things had progressed the way they were going, Wilson could have granted Rhodesia independence while stating that it could not join the Commonwealth until it had stopped being an apartheid state. That would have allowed Rhodesia to develop at its own pace, while retaining an incentive for it to allow black Africans to eventually vote. Rhodesia could have used the next few decades to develop a black African middle class.[7]

This is where Canada comes in.

Nice continent. It'd be a shame if something... happened to it.

The Prime Minister of Canada at the time, Lester B. Pearson, decided that ***Apartheid Was Unacceptable***. So he got up on his high-horse, and drafted a UN resolution committing Wilson to what was referred to as No Independence Before Majority Rule. This resolution would make it so that Rhodesia would not gain legal independence from Britain until it allowed the majority (black) population to vote. If Rhodesia were to declare independence unilaterally, international sanctions and ostracization would be imposed on it. Wilson, already facing pressure from the Queen and several other countries, agreed to sign the Canadian resolution. Rhodesia declared unilateral independence shortly thereafter, which was met with heavy international sanctions.

Now, you would think that, given the fact that Rhodesia was completely landlocked, and less than a dozen countries willing to trade with it at the time, Rhodesia would quickly collapse economically. In fact, the opposite happened. They experienced an economic boom that lasted until all of the neighbouring African countries became hostile to them. The Soviet-backed Zambia supported communist rebels in Rhodesia, and conflicts between those rebels and the government became the Rhodesian Bush War. Rhodesia eventually succumbed to international pressure abroad and guerrilla warfare within its borders, and in 1980 Rhodesia was replace by Zimbabwe, led by Robert Mugabe. Zimbabwe is awful. I won't go into all of the things that are awful about Zimbabwe, it's just too depressing.[8]

"No white person will be allowed to own land" in Zimbabwe says Mugabe; "Whites will never come back".

by Steve Goode • July 4, 2014 • 16 Comments

Mugabe begs whites to return to Zimbabwe

Category: World Published: 03 August 2015 Written by M. Crow 1898

Zimbabwe pleads for $1.5bn in food aid to prevent mass starvation

By Vasudevan Sridharan
February 10, 2016 05:30 GMT

Clearly much better than "The Breadbasket of Africa"

Now, you might be thinking that the two events are unrelated. Maybe Zimbabwe just happened to have a really bad year immediately after Mugabe kicked out the last of the white farmers.

Nope. Those white farmers moved to Zambia[9] immediately to the north of Zimbabwe, and, well...

2015

As Zambia's record harvest bursts its granaries, neighbours Botswana, Malawi and Zimbabwe stare at hunger

Zambia set to sell maize from record crop as output outstrips domestic demand.

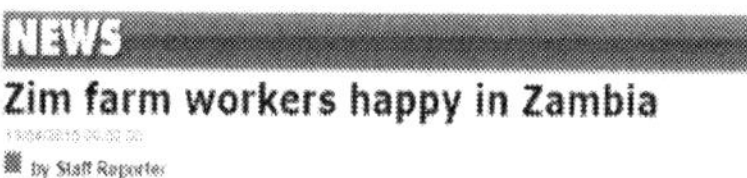

Zim farm workers happy in Zambia

by Staff Reporter

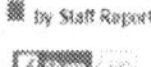
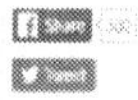

ZIMBABWEAN farm workers who lost their jobs following government's seizure of white owned farms and then migrated to neighbouring Zambia together with their bosses have said their lives have since improved.

Most white commercial farmers who were dispossessed of their farms during the height of the controversial land reform programme fled to neighbouring countries where they have reportedly set up successful farming ventures.

The bulk of the dispossessed farmers have mostly settled in Zambia's prime agricultural areas of Mazabuka, Mkushi and Mpika in Muchinga province.

RELATED STORIES

2016

Zambia expects surplus maize production despite severe drought

By

Pure Coincidence.

So, that's essentially it. Because the Canadian Prime Minister drafted a resolution and pressured the British Prime Minister to not recognize Rhodesian independence, Rhodesia eventually fell. Because Rhodesia was no longer there as a trading partner and a buffer, South Africa eventually fell. And South Africa falling was the end of a modernized, successful Africa. Had none of this happened, it is possible (not incredibly likely, but possible) that Rhodesia and South Africa could have developed black middle classes, successfully transitioned into post-apartheid states, and become the models that a successful Africa could be built on.

Other African countries might have realized that maybe, MAYBE, the decisions these countries were making were not magically working because the leaders were racist, but because the leaders were building on literally millennia of civilization that Sub-Saharan Africa simply did not go through. Maybe some of those other countries could have asked the leaders in Rhodesia and South Africa for advice.

Maybe, after a couple of decades of this, the life expectancy_in Africa could rise from 60. (For reference, the next lowest life expectancy for a continent is Asia with 72. Yes, a 12 year difference. And Africa as a whole is boosted by having semi-developed countries in the North. Sub-Saharan Africa is much, much worse).

Maybe then the world wouldn't have to spend 46 billion dollars per year in aid to Africa. Maybe.

But we'll never know.

Because of Canada.

I'll end this the same way as I plan to end each of the Blame Canada For... posts.

I'm Sorry.

[6] This is an idea explored more generally in a Moldbug essay available here: http://unqualified-reservations.blogspot.ca/2007/08/against-political-freedom.html. I would love to summarize it, but there's no way I could do it justice in a footnote.

[7] Watch this video to get an idea of why having a middle class is absolutely crucial: https://www.youtube.com/watch?v=-4SS8uyhQnY. The video is about South Africa, but the arguments are essentially identical.

[8] Read the Wikipedia page if you don't believe me: https://en.wikipedia.org/wiki/Zimbabwe.

[9] http://www.nytimes.com/2004/03/21/world/zimbabwe-s-white-farmers-start-anew-in-zambia.html

NEOCONSERVATIVES

I once heard Neoconservatives described as "liberals in slow motion." I'm not sure where, but the person who said it was undoubtedly referring to the fact that what Neoconservatives try to "conserve" is the world as it was 10 or 20 years ago, or even just the world as it is now. The problem with this, for conservatives and the right generally, is that the world of 10 or 20 years ago was very nearly as liberal as the world of today in the grand scheme of things.

Saying that Neocons are "liberals" is not even pejorative. The father of Neoconservatism, Irving Kristol, described a Neocon as "a liberal who has been mugged by reality."

History

Neoconservatism came about (and this is a gross oversimplification but is essentially accurate) when the American Left became insufficiently pro-Israel.[10] The liberals who were pro-Civil Rights Movement, pro-New Deal, pro-(essentially everything liberal up to that point) felt that the Democrats no longer supported the thing most important to them, Israel. So they jumped ship to the Republicans. But instead of integrating into the pre-existing community, they remained separate, and eventually took over the Republican party.

This is not a new phenomenon, you can see echoes of this throughout history.

If you would like a history of how Neocons took over the Republican Party, Vox Day's article[11] (and book) on who killed conservatism are essential. I disagree with the scorn that Vox places on William F. Buckley, as I think that Buckley simply made a mistake, whereas the other two people Vox blames seemed to have gotten Conservatism exactly where they wanted it. However, whether Buckley "meant to" or not is largely irrelevant, his actions did lead to the

takeover of the Republican party by Neocons. This article is not, however, a history lesson. This article is about how useful it really is to understanding Neocons to describe them as some kind of liberals.
There are three things that suddenly make a lot more sense when you understand that Neocons are liberals: Academia, The News Media, and how Republicans deal with forces hostile to them.

Academia

At the most, "conservatives" in academia make up 20%[12] of professors. That seems awfully high. I'm not sure if anyone else has taken classes at a college or university, but I can think of possibly one or two (out of dozens) of professors who actually had a problem with the general liberal worldview. On the other hand, I would say that around 20% of professors I know would have supported, for example, the Iraq war. And that's exactly it. Of the 20% of "conservative" professors, probably 90% of those are neoconservatives. That explains why "conservatives" exist in any respectable numbers at all in academia. Because Neoconservatives are really liberals, they fit in with the rest of the liberals on campus. The other 2% of professors are the actual conservatives, people like Gregory Cochran and James Watson, people genius enough that doing away with them without excuse would be overly harmful to the college in question. Until, that is, there's a large enough controversy that they can be done away with.

The News Media

Liberals control the vast majority of the news media, in the same way they control the vast majority of academia. But again, around 20% (Fox, basically) is "conservative." Why nearly complete control, instead of complete control? The answer, once again, is that the vast majority of people on Fox are Neoconservatives. Some aren't, in the same way some professors aren't, but the vast majority are. They're not driven from the field, because they agree with the liberals that control the rest of the media on most issues, even if they don't realize it.

"BUT BILL!" you cry, "Sure, it's a neat theory, but these are just your guesses, you don't have any stats to back this up. Won't you give us something juicer?"

Yes, I will. No stats though. These are just postulates.

How Republicans Deal With Hostile Forces

This is the interesting one. Liberals tend to deal with hostile outside forces (Muslims is the current example) by appeasement. They hope that by showing how kind and loving they are, the "hostile outside forces" will become "loving inside friends." It really, really, really_doesn't work.[13] But they keep trying. Maybe if they prostrate themselves just that little bit more, the other side will start playing nice. I hope you can see the parallels I'm drawing. This is exactly the strategy that modern Republicans use against Democrats. Because Neoconservatives are liberals. They see Democrats as the hostile outside force that can be won over through prostration, as opposed to how Democrats see them, as a rival that must be beaten at any cost. So Republicans swerve.[14] Because Neoconservatives are liberals.

What all this means is, **don't be surprised if Neocons get absorbed into Hillary's party.** Because Hillary is a big fan of Israel, and that's where they always belonged.[15]

---

[10] Read through this set of Irving Kristol quotes to get a sense of the intellectual underpinnings that Neoconservatism was built on: https://en.wikiquote.org/wiki/Irving_Kristol.

[11] https://voxday.blogspot.ca/2016/06/who-killed-conservatism.html

[12] http://dailysignal.com/2016/01/14/liberal-professors-outnumber-conservative-faculty-5-to-1-academics-explain-why-this-matters/

[13] Think Rotherham, Cologne, Orlando...

[14] Nick Land has a theory that politics is essentially chicken. Liberals do well, because they know they're playing chicken, so they go all out, hoping the other side will blink. Conservatives, for some reason, seem to think they're playing the iterated prisoner's dilemma. They expect that if they swerve this time, next time the liberals will cooperate with them. Obviously, this strategy does not work well when playing chicken.

[15] This would have been an impressive prediction months ago when I started writing this and got bored, before all of the Neocons started endorsing Hillary.

WAGE SLAVERY

Someone close to me kept referring to "having a job" as "slavery" and it started to bother me. And it bothered me because I had never heard someone give a rebuttal to this argument that wasn't at least 100 pages. So here goes.

Humans require things to live. Things like food, shelter, clothes, etc.

Blistering sax solos

You could, if you are a burly and intelligent man, make all of those things for yourself. You could grow crops, farm animals, shear sheep for wool, make a log cabin, keep up on repairs, and on and on.

For many people, that would take up the vast majority of your time. You probably wouldn't have time to do any of the things you want to do.

The solution that people came up with to this problem is called "division of labour".

Essentially, you find the thing you are best at that is most in demand by other people. Then you spend a certain amount of time per day doing that thing, usually less time than you would doing all the other things. All of the other people do the same thing. You then trade the time you spend doing what you're good at, for the other people doing what they're good at. Since you only have to do one thing, you can do it faster and better than you would be able to if it was one of a hundred things you had to do. Since everyone is doing that, everything gets made faster and better than it would be otherwise.

Your eight hours of skilled labour (your job) is worth twelve to fourteen hours of unskilled labour (you doing everything yourself). That leaves you with an extra four to six hours a day to do whatever you want.

Now, this is not for everyone. There are people who would be much happier taking the first option and doing everything yourself. If that person is you, then go and do that. Here_is_some free land you can have.[16] A large number of the skills you would need to survive can be found here.[17] That's fine. Nothing wrong with that.

Nothing at all...

For the people who don't find doing everything yourself all that appealing, then division of labour is your only option. At least until robots take over all the jobs. Or ultra-advanced, emulated humans.[18] Or there's a UBI and everything is magically done for us.[19]

None of this is meant to imply that the current system is ideal, or even good. All I am saying here is that a job is not slavery. It's just trading your time for other people's time.

Reading list for those wanting to know more:

Wealth of Nations by Adam Smith will get you most of the information you could possibly want on this topic.

Capital by Karl Marx is in many ways a rebuttal to Smith, but I felt Marx missed some key points.

And Human Action by Ludwig von Mises, which rebuts Marx's rebuttal.

Just about every economics book you can find will devote at least some time to division of labour. I'm not going to list all of them.[20]

---

[16].http://www.telegraph.co.uk/news/worldnews/australiaandthepacific/pitcairnislands/11418280/Why-will-nobody-move-to-Pitcairn-the-Pacific-island-with-free-land.html, http://www.aol.com/article/2010/10/19/click-here-for-free-land-five-places-where-land-is-free/19604666/, http://www.theloop.ca/9-canadian-towns-where-you-might-be-able-to-score-free-land/, http://www.theplaidzebra.com/here-are-some-places-where-you-can-get-land-for-free/, http://homesteadandprepper.com/modern-homesteading-4-places-where-land-is-free/, https://www.rt.com/politics/338775-duma-committee-approves-bill-introducing/

[17] http://www.artofmanliness.com/2015/09/28/100-skills-every-man-should-know/, http://www.thesurvivalistblog.net/tools-tips-living-land/

[18] http://ageofem.com/

[19] Universal Basic Income. Basically getting money for being alive. For a defence of it, see http://slatestarcodex.com/2014/05/23/ssc-gives-a-graduation-speech/

[20] See https://en.wikipedia.org/wiki/Division_of_labour#Further_reading

MEME MAGIC, TRUMP, AND GRANT MORRISON

Hey.

You notice things are... weird lately? Like something's a little off? Things are happening that just don't make sense?

Yeah. Me too.

When did it start happening for you? For me, it started happening in May of 2015. At the beginning of the month, I was rejected from the backup to my backup graduate school choice. This made sense. My marks weren't great, and it was not the first school to reject me. In fact, there was only one school left that had not yet responded to me. It was the top school I applied to though, so I assumed they just had a backlog.

That was not the case. I was accepted into my top choice, after being rejected from the backup to my backup. That did not make sense. It happened on June 8th. Remember that date.

Since then, I've been noticing more and more things not making sense. ISIS doesn't make sense. The refugee crisis doesn't make sense. Donald Trump's campaign doesn't make sense. Bernie Sander's campaign doesn't make sense. Rachel Dolezal doesn't make sense. Nothing going on in Sweden makes sense. Leicester City and the Toronto Blue Jays don't make sense.

Whatever's going on here also doesn't make sense.

Why is all of this happening?
I don't know. I have no idea. It's probably just a bunch of coincidences and our brains seeing patterns where there are none.

...

But what if...

...

What if Grant Morrison broke the universe?

The shirt is a bit of a giveaway.

Hypercrisis

Grant Morrison has been trying to fundamentally alter the universe for years now. It started with him taking a trip into the world of comics (somewhat literally) in Animal Man. He later put out a trilogy of books, referred to by those in the know as the Hypersigil Trilogy, consisting of Flex Mentallo, The Invisibles, and The Filth, that was intended to explore the ways that comics could affect real life. Grant Morrison is a firm believer in sigil magic. He believes that words and symbols can have power over the real world. His Hypersigil Trilogy was his attempt to use the medium of comics to try to alter his own life, he claims that it worked.

It didn't bring back that glorious hair though.

Next, Morrison used the DC Universe to try and make the real world more like the comic book world (or possibly to make the DC universe LITERALLY come to life. It's complicated). You know, where the good guys always win in the end, the bad guys are clearly bad, and things are generally more fun. This segment of his work is known as the Hypercrisis (Although the name Hypercrisis didn't originate on 4chan's /co/ board, its current usage was popularised there). Because of some things that went on at DC, it looked as if the Hypercrisis hadn't worked. That is, until Multiversity.

Multiversity

BAM!

Multiversity is an eight part comic series that explores many of the universes within the DC multiverse. But it was also Morrison's attempt to make a real life superhero. There isn't really space here (or anywhere, really) to explain how that was supposed to work. Suffice it to say, it was supposed to culminate in the issue Ultra

Comics, which is incredibly meta, and Morrison insists it's haunted. At the end (or middle. It's really meta), the superhero escapes the pages of the comic into the reader. I propose that this actually happened, and the interdimensional rip is what causes "meme magic".

What he said.

Coincidence?

Ultraa Comics came out on March 25th. The first event I know of as being described as the work of "meme magic" was the plane crash in Bains, France. There were a number of things about the crash that were strikingly similar to the prologue of The Dark Knight Rises, possibly the most memed film sequence on the internet.[21]

The date of the crash?

March 24th. One day before Ultraa Comics. Almost like a birth pang.

Trump

Donald Trump announced his campaign on June 16th, 84 days after Ultra Comics came out and 48 days after the final issue of Multiversity came out. The number 8 is one of the major recurring themes of Multiversity. The first issue of Multiversity was released in August specifically because it is the eighth month. Since his announcement, Trump has defied all expectations, and done what seemed utterly impossible. He's also been the focus of an absolute ton of times when memes have seemingly entered real life. His friendly relationship with Putin was preceded by months of memes on 4chan about how the two would get along. Trump retweeted a Pepe. Ben Garrison becoming rabidly pro-Trump. Building a wall. Bombing the shit out of ISIS. All his predictions that are mocked, then come true. And I repeat: Trump winning.

HE RETWEETED A PEPE!!!

Trump is the superhero that Grant Morrison unleashed on the world. And the world is turning into a comic book around him. Is there a more evil bad guy than ISIS? They burn people alive and film it. They're a supervillain straight out of a comic. Is there a more clearly corrupt politician in Washington than Hillary Clinton? If there is, I don't know them. Everything is becoming bright and unmuddled before our eyes.

You can dislike Trump. There are people in Action Comics who hate Superman. It happens. But he is a comic book superhero, given life by Grant Morrison.

So when you next hear someone talking about meme magic being real, remember that they might be right.

Oh. And my acceptance was on June 8th, which is 40(8X5) days after the last issue of Multiversity, and 8 days before Trump's announcement.

---

[21] This video has some highlights: https://youtu.be/aW0otG1buB8

TAKING RAP LYRICS TOO SERIOUSLY, PART 1

"Man shall not live by bread alone" –Matthew 4:4

Likewise, Northern Reaction shall not live on Right Wing Canadiana and Memeology alone. So, to show I have no idea how to appeal to an audience, I present a new series: Taking Rap Lyrics Too Seriously. Wherein I will actually answer the nonsensical questions and respond to the nonsensical statements made in rap songs.

The first lyric comes from the song Niggas in Paris by Jay-Z and Kanye West.

The Lyrics to be taken too seriously

Near the beginning of the song, Jay-Z asks:

"What's fifty grand to a motherfucker like me, can you please remind me?"

I'm pretty sure anyone in those glasses can figure it out for themselves.

Yes Mr. Z. Yes I can remind you.

The Set-Up

To keep things consistent, almost all the stats used here come from Forbes. That way the data collection methodology shouldn't skew any of the results one way or another.

The data, where available, comes originally from official government sources in 2011. That's the year the song came out, and I assume that's the year Jay-Z was interested in when he asked the question. However, Mr. Hova, if you are reading this and had another year in mind, please contact me and I will update the article accordingly.

Finally, instead of using averages, I will be using medians, just in case the groups in question are either top-heavy (think 1%ers) or bottom-heavy (massive credit card debt, etc.)

The Math

To calculate what "50 grand" is to a "motherfucker" like Jay-Z, we need to know a few things. First, how much is Jay-Z worth?

According to Forbes,[22] in 2011, Jay-Z was the second richest rapper alive after Diddy, with a net worth of $450,000,000. That's a lot of money.

The physician known as "Dre" came in third. Sad, because he's got those medical school debts to pay off.

With that figure in mind, "50 grand" would be 1/9000 of Jay-Z's total net worth.

Next, we need something to compare it to.

The median income in America in 2011 was $52,000.[23] If we take that number and divide it by 9000, we get 5.7777...

So, fifty grand to Jay-Z is the equivalent of $5.78 to the median American.

But we can go deeper.

Jay-Z is black.

I was surprised too.

The median net worth of black Americans and white Americans is very different, for a variety of reasons.[24]

The median net worth of a white American was $111,000 in 2011.[25] Doing the same calculation as before, fifty grand to Jay-Z is like $12.30 to the median white American.

The median net woth of black Americans in 2011 was just $9000.[26] See above for some of the reasons why. Using the math one more time, fifty grand to Jay-Z is like $1 to the median black American.

Conclusion

Mr. Jigga, you asked us to remind you what fifty grand was to a motherfucker like you.

Every time you buy an 18k gold men's Rolex watch, that's like the median American buying a Venti Pumpkin Spice Latte from Starbucks. Every time you buy a brand new Audi A5 with a sunroof, that's like the median white American buying a ticket to see a movie. And every time you buy a new yacht, that's the equivalent of the median black American buying a can of soup.

So there you have it. To a motherfucker like you, fifty grand is not a lot.

Well you don't have to rub it in.

---

[22] http://www.forbes.com/sites/zackomalleygreenburg/2011/03/09/the-forbes-five-hip-hop-wealthiest-artists/

[23] https://publications.credit-suisse.com/tasks/render/file/index.cfm?fileid=88E41853-83E8-EB92-9D5895A42B9499B1

[24] Some believe it's due to genetics, some culture, some policy, and some think it's a remnant of previous policy. I have no idea the answer.

[25] http://www.forbes.com/sites/laurashin/2015/03/26/the-racial-wealth-gap-why-a-typical-white-household-has-16-times-the-wealth-of-a-black-one/

[26] See previous note.

DON'T PUNCH RIGHT

(This is taken from a Twitter rant I went on earlier. I may expand on it at some point.)

Ok, something has been bugging me for a while. People on the Alt-Right need to understand the meaning of "Never Punch Right", also known as "No enemies on the right, no friends on the left."

The idea behind that is that anyone doing something to the right of you is "Good" and anyone doing something to the left of you is "Bad". It does NOT mean "Don't punch anyone ON the right", because that would not allow us to criticise people like Paul Ryan or Ted Cruz. Those people are on "The Right" as it currently stands in the American political spectrum, but they are to the left of you and I. "Criticise anyone not exactly as right as me" is cuckservative logic and doesn't work. "Don't criticise anyone on the right" encourages a leftward shift as more and more "somewhat right-wing" people are accepted into what I will call the "mainstream Alt-Right" while noting the irony of that phrase. The only effective strategy, the one leftists have perfected, is to not criticise anyone to the right of you. This pushes the Overton Window to the right.

So if you see someone criticise Milo because He's gay or something, don't defend Milo unless Milo is to the right of you and the criticism is coming from the left. Because criticism directed at Milo for being insufficiently right-wing pushes the Overton Window in the same way Milo's existence does. Yes, Milo is probably pushing the mainstream further right on some issues, but defending him does nothing to further the cause besides allowing the cause to move leftward.

That does not necessarily mean you have to actively engage in criticism of Milo. I don't always. But it does mean that you should let those to the right of you do it. Because that's what works.

Now, there are two points of contention in this strategy that need working out. First, how does being an IRL activist affect how far "right" you are. Should someone slightly to the left of you be immune from your criticism because they stage protests (or whatever) and you're an ideologue only? I have no idea. Something to think about. The other hiccup is how far that criticism should go? I personally think that the action against the person should be directly proportional to how far to the right of the person you are. Basically any (legal) action against Paul Ryan is fine, because he's way off to the Left of us. Someone else in the movement? Trolling/criticism should maybe be the extent of it. But again, it depends how far to the left of you they are.

I'm basically done now.

Tl;dr, Punch ON the right, don't punch TO YOUR right.

PARODUS CANADIANUS

If you don't know anything about Canada, when you think of "Canadian Identity" or "Canadian Culture" you probably think of snow, beavers, maple syrup, legal weed, and hockey.

Maybe bagged milk.

If you live in Canada, or if you've been watching Justin Trudeau, you've probably heard that Canada has no Identity or Culture, besides Multiculturalism™.

I'm here to tell you why that's bullshit.

Types of Multiculturalism

There are three relevant types of multiculturalism, and it's important to understand the differences between them in order to understand Canadian multiculturalism.

The first type is the American model, also known as the Melting Pot theory. Essentially, everyone comes to America with their own cultures, but they assimilate into American culture. If there's something really great about their culture, it might become a part of American culture. There are pros and cons to this type of multiculturalism, but this article is not the place for that discussion.[27]

The second type of multiculturalism, the kind that is pushed for regularly in Canada, is the Salad Bowl theory. It argues that Canada has no distinct culture of its own, and that "Canadian" culture is just the patchwork of cultures that each person brings to Canada. This is an awful system for a number of reasons, most notably because it emphasizes the differences between peoples that leads to the loss of social cohesion discussed in Robert Putnam's landmark study on diversity.[28]

To be clear, any kind of diversity will decrease social cohesion and trust. But the Salad Bowl theory, instead of passively allowing the differences that lead to social friction to exist, actively promotes those differences as the most important thing in society. Society is like a family. The Melting Pot is like that family adopting a child. The Salad Bowl is like polyamory[29]: if everyone involved is a High-IQ Homo Economicus[30] then it might work out, but if not, you are just ruining everything for everyone.

The third type of multiculturalism is the kind that Canada was founded on, and actually explains a lot of the odd things about Canada. There isn't a name for this kind of multiculturalism as far as I know, so I will refer to it as Garrison Multiculturalism for reasons that will become clear shortly.

No, He's from Montana, not Canada.

Whereas Melting Pot has all of the different cultures converging into one culture, Garrison Multiculturalism has the cultures remaining separate. After a few generations, an Italian-American family becomes simply an American family. An Italian-Canadian family remains an Italian-Canadian family. The difference between Garrison Multiculturalism and the Salad Bowl is that Garrison Multiculturalism insists that the cultures coming to Canada adopt certain aspects of Canadian culture, whereas the Salad Bowl does not.

There are two origins of Garrison Multiculturalism, the boring one and the interesting one. The boring one is that when Canada was founded, there were three cultures, all insisting on their own continued existence: British, French, and Native. The solution our founders came to was to agree that all three cultures were distinct but equally Canadian. As I said, this is the boring answer. But the question now is, why was that the solution the founders came to, instead of the American model or some other solution? The answer to that brings us to the interesting origin of Garrison Multiculturalism: The Garrison Mentality.

Still no.

Garrison Mentality

The Garrison Mentality is a term coined by Northrop Frye, perhaps the best literary critic of the 20th century, to explain a running theme in Canadian literature. It was expanded upon somewhat by Margaret Atwood, but it was still confined to Canadian literature. I propose that the Garrison Mentality actually explains many aspects of Canadian culture, including our multiculturalism.

The Garrison Mentality refers to the fact that during the early years of Canada, the winters were extremely harsh, so everyone would spend the winter huddled together in the local fort (or garrison). In the summer they would have their own homes, but the winters were too cold for individuals to go it alone. Frye argues that cultural memories of these times inspired Canadian writers to use the theme of Man vs. Nature much more than American authors, who focused on Man vs. Man and Man vs. Himself. But this idea also explains so much about Canadians generally. Why are Canadians so polite? Because the person you are rude to might be the one with the last spare blanket when winter comes. Why are Canadians accepting of other cultures? Because who cares if the guy with a hot bowl of soup down the street speaks English or French, as long as you can communicate "Do you have any extra?" to him.

This does not, however, imply a blanket acceptance of all other peoples no matter what, like we're led to believe by the Salad Bowl proponents. The unstated implication of the Garrison Mentality is that there are consequences to not going along. Think of it like the iterated prisoner's dilemma.[31] The Garrison Mentality has the first prisoner cooperating no matter what on the first two turns, but after that matching whatever the second prisoner did on the previous turn.

So Canadians try not to piss anyone off (cooperating on the first turn). If someone bumps into a Canadian (defects on the first turn), the Canadian will apologize (cooperating on the second turn). If the stranger tells the apologizing Canadian to "fuck off" at that point (defecting on the second turn), the Canadian will respond in kind by telling the stranger to "take off, eh?" (defecting on the third turn). If the stranger then apologizes for the misunderstanding (cooperating on the third turn), the Canadian will also apologize (cooperating on the fourth turn) and will continue to cooperate for as long as the stranger does as well.

The macro point to all of this is that the Garrison Mentality means that Canadians cooperate with those willing to cooperate. The Canadian is not just the man apologizing for fear of offending the man with the last spare blanket, he is also the man with the last spare blanket willing to not share if he is sufficiently offended. If there is no fear of repercussions, there is nothing stopping everyone defecting all the time, taking advantage of the cooperating Canadians.

This, then, is the difference between Salad Bowl and Garrison Multiculturalism. Salad Bowl teaches Canadians to cooperate no matter what, which leads to outside groups taking advantage of the willingness to cooperate. Garrison Multiculturalism teaches Canadians to give people the benefit of the doubt, and after that cooperate with them as long as they are willing to cooperate with you. Anyone can become a Canadian, as long as they are willing and able to cooperate in this way. If they are not, then they are not Canadian, they are just taking advantage of Canada.

So when you hear about Canada being built on multiculturalism, don't picture Toronto, divided up into ethnic enclaves, presided over by the Rootless Cosmopolitan Justin Trudeau, ensuring by force that no one is subject to disparate impact.[32] Picture a Frenchman, an Iroquois, and an Englishman sharing their last blanket and a pot of soup, because if they didn't, all three would die. They don't like the fact that they're different, they tolerate that fact because survival is more important. But if one of them started refusing to pull his own weight...

---

[27] John Derbyshire has a decent article that touches on the topic here: http://www.vdare.com/articles/john-derbyshire-on-why-race-realism-makes-more-sense-than-magic-dirt-theory

[28] Available here: http://macaulay.cuny.edu/eportfolios/benediktsson2013/files/2013/04/Putnam.pdf

[29] Essentially having lots of different relationships at once, and everyone's cool with it.

[30] A person who is intelligent, has a low time preference (is able to delay gratification), and is satisfied with gaining material wealth.

[31] The prisoner's dilemma goes like this: Imagine two prisoners are being interrogated separately. Each has the option to either cooperate with the other by staying silent, or defect against the other by snitching. If they both stay silent, they both get one year in jail. If one snitches, he gets no time, the other guy gets three years. If they both snitch on each other, they both get two years. The iterated version of the prisoner's dilemma is just the above, but repeated for either a specified or unspecified number of times.

[32] Same input, different results. For example, requiring that all firefighters be over six feet tall would have a disparate impact on women wanting to be firefighters, since there are far fewer women over six feet than men.

EXCURSIONS AROUND THE RIGHT #1

I've been meaning to do shorter, more frequent posts in addition to the longer ones. So I'm starting "Excursion Around The Right."[33]

First up, an article by Thomas Barghest on Social Matter.[34] Read it. It's long, but worth it.

I only wanted to add one point to it.

The article quotes Francis Fukuyama on Plato's conception of the soul:

"[Plato said] there were three parts to the soul, a desiring part, a reasoning part, and a part that he called *thymos*, or "spiritedness." Much of human behavior can be explained as a combination of the first two parts, desire and reason: desire induces men to seek things outside themselves, while reason or calculation shows them the best way to get them. But in addition, human beings seek recognition of their own worth, or of the people, things, or principles that they invest with worth... The desire for recognition, and the accompanying emotions of anger, shame, and pride, are parts of the human personality critical to the political life."

Fukuyama (building on Nietzsche) says that liberal democracy molds people into men without *Thymos*, also referred to as Men without Chests. The article goes on to apply this to our current political climate:

"The alt-right insult "cuckservative" is directed precisely at these men without chests. Trump, on the other hand, is a perfect example of a man of *thymos*, a man with a broad chest and "high energy," who again and again confounds the expectations of this era's best approximations of last men."

This analysis of Trump struck me like a hammer blow, because it pinpointed the exact moment in history when I stopped being simply entertained by Trump, and when I started being fully on his side. That exact moment was during the speech with Trump's famous interaction with Jorge Ramos. But it wasn't the wonderful flippancy of "Go back to Univision" that sold me on Trump. It was this line:

"We're going to get things back in shape. This country's gonna be so strong and so great, and you're gonna be so **proud** of it."

That word right there. Proud. Trump used the word many times before and since, saying the voters will be "Proud of him" and that he'll "make you Proud to be an American again."

At the time, that struck me as an idea in politics I couldn't remember ever hearing before, at least not recently. Can you imagine Hillary saying "I'm going to make you so proud"? I can't. If you search "Hillary Clinton Make You Proud" without quotes, you get two types of results. First, Hillary saying she's "proud to be ____" which is exactly the opposite of an aspirational phrase. The other type of result is articles about Trump. That says something.

Trump's use of the idea of pride, I think, is exactly the kind of thing Thomas Barghest was talking about in the Social Matter article. An appeal not to the mind, or the gut, but the chest.

Was anyone else struck by Trump's use of "Proud" throughout the campaign? Does this seem like an adequate explanation?

---

[33] The name is a play on the song Excursion Around The Bay by Great Big Sea.

[34] Available here: http://www.socialmatter.net/2016/08/26/say-america-not-communist-country/

A METAPOLITICAL DEFENSE OF MILO

Semi-serious disclaimer: Milo Yiannopoulos is a gay, Jewish, mostly libertarian miscegenist who needs to be purged.[35] He should not be allowed anywhere near the leadership of the Alt-Right.

What This Is Not

This is not a political defense of Milo. Milo shares very few views with the vast majority of the Alt-Right, and does not belong among them. Everyone on the Alt-Right is absolutely correct in being terribly upset that Milo is often the person the media pretend is the leader of the Alt-Right. Milo needs to be punched from the Right, often and hard.[36]

"Curly Headed Fuck" -Will Farrell.

That being said, he's never claimed to be a member of the Alt-Right, has he? In fact, he's very careful to always refer to the Alt-Right as "they" and "them." He's referred to as a "leader" of the Alt-Right by other journalists, but journalists are by and large idiots who hate nuance on the right. And this is not simply his journalistic impartiality. He had no qualms about saying he was a member of gamergate. So let's assume, for the sake of argument, that Milo does not consider himself a member of the Alt-Right. What the hell is he doing?

The easy answer is that he's looking for a quick cash grab. He's latching onto something no one else will latch onto, and as such he gets the massive publicity associated with a move like that. But it's not quite as simple as that. Milo isn't just covering the Alt-Right, he's covering them using positive, sometimes glowing terms.

He covers the Alt-Right the way Sally fucking Kohn talks about Black Lives Matter.[37]

He has nothing but praise for most of the Alt-Right's goals, and, for the most part, when he talks about the "Extremists," he gives a sort of "they're not really serious, boys will be boys" defense. Which is, again, exactly what Sally Kohn says about BLM. She says that the vast majority of the movement is good, and that the violent thugs are either not really part of the movement, or "venting their frustration" or some other such nonsense. There are two metapolitical strategies being employed by both Sally and Milo. Milo's use of these strategies is why, although he's politically wrong and bad and should be spat upon (see disclaimer), he's a metapolitical role model for the Alt-Right, and you should all take notes.

Strategy 1: Motte and Bailey

The Motte and Bailey strategy is a bit complicated, but works REALLY well.[38] Basically you have two versions of the same argument, the motte version, and the bailey version. When you're pushing for policy changes, or trying to get anything done, you use the lush, fertile bailey argument. The problem with the bailey argument is that it doesn't hold up to the least bit of scrutiny. So if you encounter the least bit of scrutiny, you retreat to your motte argument. The motte argument is essentially impregnable, but useless for actually getting anything you want out of the argument.

The "classic" example is feminism. Their bailey argument is "Feminism means we need to have hiring quotas and discourage motherhood and encourage promiscuity." When you say "Well then, feminism is awful," they counter with their motte argument: "Feminism is the radical notion that women are people. Since you're against feminism, you must not think women are people!" You see, if they started with the "women are people" argument, they wouldn't be able to go anywhere. There are absolutely no policies in The West that don't treat women as people. None. So saying "women should be treated like people" is the same as saying "things should continue as they do now." Feminists don't want that. So they use their bailey argument until they're called on its deficiencies and have to retreat to their motte.

What I'd like to tell to "anti feminism" people

Feminism DOESN'T demonize men.
Feminists DON'T hate men.
Feminists CARE about LGBTQ people.
Feminists CARE about men who get raped.
Feminism FIGHTS rape culture.
Feminists CARE about young girls who have to marry 45+ men.
Feminists CARE about E V E R Y B O D Y

FEMINISM MEANS EQUALITY, NOT "GIRL POWER".

#feminism #feminist #anti feminism

This is what a feminist motte looks like.

This is what Milo is doing with the Alt-Right. I have never seen Milo ask anyone on the Alt-Right to stop doing any of the things they're doing. The closest he came was the "1488" section of his article[39], and even there he just essentially says the 1488 crowd doesn't represent the whole movement, not that they should be purged. When Milo talks about the Alt-Right, he'll say they're valiant but maligned white men, doing their best to keep their culture alive. That they're a real political force with serious and legitimate grievances, and are incredibly savvy. That's the bailey. When another journalist points out that most on the Alt-Right post gleeful pictures of Nazi frogs gassing (((journalists))) and cry out for "RACE WAR NOW," Milo retreats to the motte: "They're just having fun, trying to get a rise out of you. Why do you hate fun?" There's no counter to that argument without sounding like a fuddy-duddy, so the Alt-Right gets to keep doing what it's doing. Milo says "They're just trolling, no one is actually anti-Semitic," and Kevin MacDonald posts another graph showing the ethnic makeup of Harvard graduates.

"It's just a prank bro" -Dr. Kevin Macdonald, on the JQ

The motte and bailey is an excellent strategy that the left has absolutely mastered with BLM (Black Lives Matter vs. reparations), Islam (Religion of Peace vs. insane speech codes so as not to offend), and trans rights (What business is it of yours what others do vs. unisex bathrooms and fines for misgendering) among many others.

It's nice to see someone on the right doing it so deftly.

Now, you may worry that this marginalizes the rightward fringes of the movement, like Republicans disavowing the John Birch Society. But what Milo is doing is different than that. He is not calling out specific people or subsets of the movement, he is vaguely gesturing at a boogeyman for the media to worry about, while claiming most of the Alt-Right is an ideology of peace. How has that worked out in regards to Islam? Every time someone in the media says Muslims reject violence, it just encourages the violent Muslims to be more violent. And since Islam (and the Alt-Right) is definitionally sympathetic to the most extremist elements of the movement, that increased extremism will be embraced as well.

But why would Milo want to be supportive of those extremists on the Alt-Right? Many are far more anti-gay and anti-Semitic than anyone in the Republican party ever was, which isn't exactly good for him.

This brings me to the second metapolitical strategy that Milo is employing: Don't Punch Right.

Strategy 2: Don't Punch Right

I've spoken on this before, so I won't dwell on the point. Milo, again, is some kind of conservative libertarian. He advocates for his position, as seen in his gay meet-ups and other things like that. But crucially, he defends the Alt-Right because the Alt-Right is to the right of him. He understands that normalizing the Alt-Right makes his position seem much more moderate by comparison. That's the whole point of Don't Punch Right. You defend (or at the very least tolerate) anyone to the right of you so that the Overton Window moves to the right. Milo would not be happy in the world that many in the Alt-Right want, but he knows that it's in the direction that he wants, so he normalizes it.

Conclusion

Milo is wrong politically (again, see the disclaimer). But, for the most part, he is doing the right things metapolitically. Don't emulate Milo's views, but many in the Alt-Right would do well to learn from his strategies. Don't do as Milo does, do as he meta-does.

(This may also apply, to one degree or another, to many the members of the so-called "Alt-Lite": Paul Joseph Watson, Lauren Southern, Mike Cernovich, Gavin McInnes, Pizza Party Ben, and keep moving right until you're satisfied that the person you're talking about is solidly in the Alt-Right. They're entryists that need to be purged, but they often employ the correct metapolitical strategies.)[40]

[35] Or just punched from the right. See Don't Punch Right, page

---

47.

[36] See previous note.

[37] Obsessively.

[38] You should probably read this blog post on it, I'm going to butcher the description: http://slatestarcodex.com/2014/07/07/social-justice-and-words-words-words/

[39] Available here: http://www.breitbart.com/tech/2016/03/29/an-establishment-conservatives-guide-to-the-alt-right/

[40] Time has not been kind to the above list since it was written. The only consistent one ended up being Pizza Party Ben. Odd, that.

TAKING RAP LYRICS TOO SERIOUSLY, PART 2

Part Two in Taking Rap Lyrics Too Seriously will be discussing the DMX song Where Tha Hood At? in honour of my appearance on the DMX-obsessed podcast Exodus Americanus.[41]

In this song, DMX repeatedly asks the following question:

"Where the hood, where the hood, where the hood at?"

Obviously DMX had his own reasons for asking this question.[42]

You don't know! Maybe he wants to spread the word of the lord to troubled youths!

But, like last time, let's take the question literally: Where is the hood, in relation to DMX?

Getting information on both where DMX was living at the time of the recording and where the song itself was recorded has proven difficult. However, all of the information I could find on DMX from before this song said he lived in New York City, and both of the labels that he recorded the song for (Def Jam and Ruff Ryders) are based in New York City, so it seems like a safe bet that the question was asked in New York.

Next, what does DMX mean by "hood"?

Probably not

Urban Dictionary says that "hood" refers to "ghetto", and given DMX's lengthy_legal history, it seems obvious that he meant the high-crime variety, not the "Jewish ghetto" variety. So, let's look for high crime neighbourhoods in 2003. The FBI keeps records[43] of every kind of crime you can think of everywhere, but they make it very difficult to compare all metropolitan areas by violent crime rate. So, instead, we will have to settle for cities with a population above 100,000. What we're looking for here is the "hood" with the highest crime rate per capita, and the "hood" that ranks in the top ten that is closest to DMX, all using 2003 numbers. That way DMX can choose whether he values hood-ness or proximity more when asking "Where the hood at?"
So, the top ten most violent cities in America, by violent crime rate per 100,000 people in 2003, were:

10. **St. Petersburg, Florida** with 1601.8.

9. **North Charleston, South Carolina** with 1658.2.

8. **Orlando, Florida** with 1684.

7. **Baltimore, Maryland** with 1735.

6. **Tampa, Florida** with 1786.5.

5. **Miami, Florida** with 1875.3.

4. **Springfield, Massachusetts** with 1896.1.

3. **Atlanta, Georgia** with 1969.6.

2. **Detroit, Michigan** with 2018.2.

And the most violent city is...

1. St. Louis, Missouri with a
whopping **2181.9** violent offences per 100,000
people.

Therefore, Mr. DMX, if you wanted to find the most "hood" place, St. Louis is your best bet.

However, we also need to rank these cities by proximity to where the question was asked: New York City. I will be using straight line numbers, as DMX seemed fairly desperate to find the hood, so I assume he would be willing to charter a plane to get there.

OF COURSHE!

From ranked from furthest to closest to New York (and by extension DMX in 2003), the closest hood cities are:

10. **Miami, Florida** at 1093 miles.

9. **St. Petersburg, Florida** at 1021 miles.

8. **Tampa, Florida** at 1004 miles.

7. **Orlando, Florida** at 940 miles.

6. **St. Louis, Missouri** at 872 miles.

5. **Atlanta, Georgia** at 746.

4. **North Charleston, South Carolina** at 635 miles.

3. **Detroit, Michigan** at 481 miles.

2. **Baltimore, Maryland** at 169 miles.

And the closest hood to DMX in 2003 was...

1. Springfield, Massachusetts at 102 miles.

There you have it Mr. DMX. If in 2003, when you asked "Where The Hood At?" you wanted the most hood place in America, your answer was **St. Louis, Missouri**. However, if you wanted the closest hood to you that is in the top ten most hood places in America, **Springfield, Massachusetts** was your best bet.

How does DMX feel about Luda? Because Luda's already in Springfield.

I hope this answer to the question you posed more than a decade ago proves useful to you.

---

[41] Which can be found at http://exodusamericanus.com/

[42] DMX doesn't like gay gangstas, and essentially meant "Where did all the real men go?"

[43] Available here: https://ucr.fbi.gov/crime-in-the-u.s/2003/03sec2.pdf

RE-PACKING THE INVISIBLE BACKPACK

I hate the essay *White Privilege: Unpacking the Invisible Backpack* by Peggy McIntosh.

Artist's reconstruction of Peggy.

Because it conflates many things that have nothing to do with each other, and puts them all down as "White Privilege." I'm going to break all the points Peggy makes down and categorise them as either White Privilege, or something else. And remember, if something is "White Privilege," it must

1. Not just be an encounter with some bigoted asshole.
2. Apply to all white people, and not to other races
3. Apply to a white person raised by blacks
4. Not apply to a black person raised by whites.

So, with those points in mind, let's look at the backpack:

> ***1. I can if I wish arrange to be in the company of people of my race most of the time.***

This is a product of diversity. If Peggy lived in Detroit, she would not have this privilege, but a black person would. Therefore, not white privilege.

> ***2. I can avoid spending time with people whom I was trained to mistrust and who have learned to mistrust my kind or me.***

Same as the above point, but with added passive-aggressive undertones. Peggy would not have this privilege in Detroit. Therefore, not white privilege.

> ***3. If I should need to move, I can be pretty sure of renting or purchasing housing in an area which I can afford and in which I would want to live.***

If we want to talk about privileges, this is a product of class privilege, not white privilege. Jay-Z can do this,[44] a poor white guy in rural Alabama cannot.

> ***4. I can be pretty sure that my neighbors in such a location will be neutral or pleasant to me.***

Two points here. First, like the above point, this is a product of wealth. Rich neighbourhoods are low crime neighbourhoods generally. Second, the truth of this statement will largely depend on how diverse the neighbourhood is. Low diversity neighbourhoods, black or white, are more pleasant (higher social cohesion and trust) than high diversity ones.

> ***5. I can go shopping alone most of the time, pretty well assured that I will not be followed or harassed.***

This is another example of class privilege. If Peggy was a poor white girl in Detroit, this would not be true.

6. I can turn on the television or open to the front page of the paper and see people of my race widely represented.

Now, finally, we have reached something that could be considered white privilege. Let's look at the numbers. In 2013 there was a study[45] examining racial representations in top grossing films. It found that in 2008, the racial makeup of movie characters was: 71% white and 13% black and the rest Asian, Hispanic, or other. Now, according to the US census,[46] the racial makeup of the US in 2010 (the only date around there I could find easily) was 63.7% white and 12.2% black. So, yes, whites are over represented, but **so are blacks.** All of this is a red herring though, since this would be true of any person living in any country as a minority. A white person living in Japan would experience this. We'll file this under "Racial Majority Privilege," so as not to be white-country chauvinists.

7. When I am told about our national heritage or about "civilization," I am shown that people of my color made it what it is.

Two points to be made here: First, this is another racial majority privilege, as it would be equally true for a Japanese person living in Japan.

Second, what if people of Peggy's colour actually did make it what it is? I'm not arguing here that that's the case (go read a history book), but if it were the case, I'm not sure "My ancestors did more awesome stuff than your ancestors" is what most people think they mean when they say "white privilege."

> ***8. I can be sure that my children will be given curricular materials that testify to the existence of their race.***

Oh boy. Um... Let's give Peggy the benefit of the doubt and assume that this was really the case when she wrote it. It is no longer the case. Find me one well respected professor or curriculum that includes "White Studies" in anything approaching a neutral (not even positive, but neutral) way. Now find me a major university that does not have an African American Studies department. I seriously doubt you'll be able to find either.

> ***9. If I want to, I can be pretty sure of finding a publisher for this piece on white privilege.***

That's nice Peggy. But that has nothing to do with white privilege. A random white person off the street probably couldn't get this piece published, and you couldn't get an article published called "Black Privilege" that talked about diversity hires or SAT score boosts. Maybe this has less to do with your own white privilege, and more to do with the popularity of the concept of "White Privilege".

> ***10. I can be pretty sure of having my voice heard in a group in which I am the only member of my race.***

People listen to tokens, be they white or black. In today's political climate (and depending on the issue talked about), a black person in a group of whites would probably be more listened to than Peggy in a group of blacks. This one is incredibly subjective as well.

> ***11. I can be casual about whether or not to listen to another person's voice in a group in which s/he is the only member of his/her race.***

Not if you want to keep your job you can't. Again, we'll give Peggy the benefit of the doubt and assume this was true at the time. It is no longer true.

> ***12. I can go into a music shop and count on finding the music of my race represented, into a supermarket and find the staple foods which fit with my cultural traditions, into a hairdresser's shop***

> ***and find someone who can cut my hair.***

Let's again give Peggy the benefit of the doubt and assume this was true at the time. It is no longer true. Find me a record store without a rap section, and a supermarket that sells haggis. However, even if this was true, it would still be a racial majority privilege, since it would also automatically be true of whites in China.

> ***13. Whether I use checks, credit cards or cash, I can count on my skin color not to work against the appearance of financial reliability.***

Let's ignore the unsubstantiated nature of this claim, and point out the fact that Jews and Asians are seen as (and are) richer than whites in the US. This is therefore not white privilege (remember Rule 2), but black (and maybe Latino) anti-privilege

> ***14. I can arrange to protect my children most of the time from people who might not like them.***

Class Privilege. I'm going to stop explaining these ones, they're fairly obvious.

> ***15. I do not have to educate my children to be aware of systemic racism for their own daily physical protection.***

This begs the question. "Here's a list of white privileges. One of the white privileges is that my kids don't have to learn about white privileges."

> ***16. I can be pretty sure that my children's teachers and employers will tolerate them if they fit school and workplace norms; my chief worries about them do not concern others' attitudes toward their race.***

First, tell that to Aaron.[47] Second, I don't know of one case where a black student was reprimanded for being black, while conforming to "school and workplace norms." The argument we hear now is that those norms themselves are racist because of disparate impact.

> ***17. I can talk with my mouth full and not have people put this down to my color.***

So can Asians. Black anti-privilege.

> ***18. I can swear, or dress in second hand clothes, or not answer letters, without having people attribute these choices to the bad morals, the poverty or the illiteracy of my race.***

So can Asians. Black anti-privilege.

> ***19. I can speak in public to a powerful male group without putting my race on trial.***

So can Asians? I'm not completely sure what Peggy is saying with this one, but if it's anything, it's probably Black anti-privilege.

> ***20. I can do well in a challenging situation without being called a credit to my race.***

So can Asians and Jews. Black anti-privilege.

> ***21. I am never asked to speak for all the people of my racial group.***

Racial majority privilege. If Peggy was the only white person on a school board in Detroit, she very well could be asked to speak for the white interests of the community. If anyone cared.

> ***22. I can remain oblivious of the language and customs of persons of color who constitute the world's majority without feeling in my culture any penalty for such oblivion.***

Not if you want tenure you can't. But seriously, this is another racial majority privilege. A farmer in China wouldn't feel a penalty for not knowing English. This is also less "white privilege" than Anglo privilege in the US. No one knows about Slovakian language and culture. (Sorry to my two Slovak readers).

> ***23. I can criticize our government and talk about how much I fear its policies and behavior without being seen as a cultural outsider.***

Black Lives Matter was endorsed by the president, your argument is invalid.

> ***24. I can be pretty sure that if I ask to talk to the "person in charge", I will be facing a person of my race.***

Well, probably someone Jewish.[48] But ignoring that, this is another racial majority privilege that wouldn't be true in Detroit.

> ***25. If a traffic cop pulls me over or if the IRS audits my tax return, I can be sure I haven't been singled out because of my race.***

This is not true of the IRS and it is not true of traffic stops.[49]

> ***26. I can easily buy posters, post-cards, picture books, greeting cards, dolls, toys and children's magazines featuring people of my race.***

Racial majority privilege, Though I'd be surprised if this "problem" still exists today.

> ***27. I can go home from most meetings of organizations I belong to feeling somewhat tied in, rather than isolated, out-of-place, outnumbered, unheard, held at a distance or feared.***

DIVERSITY! Ain't it great?

> ***28. I can be pretty sure that an argument with a colleague of another race is more likely to jeopardize her/his chances for advancement than to jeopardize mine.***

If this was true at the time, it is no longer true. HR departments have made firing non-whites harder than firing whites.

> ***29. I can be pretty sure that if I argue for the promotion of a person of another race, or a program centering on race, this is not likely to cost me heavily within my present setting, even if my colleagues disagree with me.***

First off, this is true for Asians as well. Second, just try to start a "white people advocacy program." I dare you.

> ***30. If I declare there is a racial issue at hand, or there isn't a racial issue at hand, my race will lend me more credibility for either position than a person of color will have.***

If this was true at the time, it is CERTAINLY no longer true. When was the last time anyone listened to a white person say "there's no racism here, move along"?

> ***31. I can choose to ignore developments in minority writing and minority activist programs, or disparage them, or learn from them, but in any case, I can find ways to be more or less protected from negative consequences of any of these choices.***

And blacks can be protected from the consequences of ignoring Russian writing and activism. This is somewhere between racial majority privilege and Anglo privilege.

> ***32. My culture gives me little fear about ignoring the perspectives and powers of people of other races.***

Except Asians. We can't piss off China. But seriously, this would also be true of a Chinese person in China. Racial majority privilege.

33. I am not made acutely aware that my shape, bearing or body odor will be taken as a reflection on my race.

"White Trash motor scooter." But seriously, I'm going to pull out Rule 1 for this one. No one but a bigotted asshole would do this, and there are plenty of bigotted asshole blacks who talk about white women smelling like wet dogs, or having thin lips.

34. I can worry about racism without being seen as self-interested or self-seeking.

Only because you're not allowed to worry about racism against whites. In which case, "self-interested and self-seeking" are very polite compared to how you would be described.

35. I can take a job with an affirmative action employer without having my co-workers on the job suspect that I got it because of my race.

This is also true of Asians, but the solution for this is "Don't have affirmative action employers," and that's the opposite of what Peggy wants.

36. If my day, week or year is going badly, I need not ask of each negative episode or situation whether it had racial overtones.

Racial majority privilege. Japanese people in Japan also don't have to worry about this.

37. I can be pretty sure of finding people who would be willing to talk with me and advise me about my next steps, professionally.

There are programs specifically designed to help blacks with employment issues. There are no programs to help just whites with employment issues, that would be racist. Also, class privilege.

38. I can think over many options, social, political, imaginative or professional, without asking whether a person of my race would be accepted or allowed to do what I want to do.

Find me a career that isn't begging for more qualified female black applicants.

> ***39. I can be late to a meeting without having the lateness reflect on my race.***

Asians and Jews, with a smattering of racial majority privilege.

> ***40. I can choose public accommodation without fearing that people of my race cannot get in or will be mistreated in the places I have chosen.***

Asians and Jews again, so black anti-privilege.

> ***41. I can be sure that if I need legal or medical help, my race will not work against me.***

There are medical and legal help funds for blacks only. There are no medical or legal help funds for whites only.

> ***42. I can arrange my activities so that I will never have to experience feelings of rejection owing to my race.***

Unless you want to play basketball in the inner city. Also, class privilege.

> ***43. If I have low credibility as a leader I can be sure that my race is not the problem.***

Also true of Jews and Asians. Black anti-privilege.

> ***44. I can easily find academic courses and institutions which give attention only to people of my race.***

No Peggy, you can't, that would be racist.

> ***45. I can expect figurative language and imagery in all of the arts to testify to experiences of my race.***

Racial majority privilege. Also, "All the arts"? What about Manga or Anime?

> ***46. I can chose blemish cover or bandages in "flesh" color and have them more or less match my skin.***

This one I have no idea about. Let's give Peggy the benefit of the doubt and say that this is, indeed, true, and that bandages worldwide are generally white flesh coloured (If this was not true worldwide, it would just be racial majority privilege again).

> ***47. I can travel alone or with my spouse without expecting embarrassment or hostility in those who deal with us.***

I seriously doubt you can do that in downtown Detroit. Racial majority privilege.

> ***48. I have no difficulty finding neighborhoods where people approve of our household.***

Class privilege.

> ***49. My children are given texts and classes which implicitly support our kind of family unit and do not turn them against my choice of domestic partnership.***

I have no idea why Peggy thought this was a white privilege. This is not true for white polygamists, but is true for "westernized" people of all colours. Isn't assuming all black people have weird family units... kinda racist?

> ***50. I will feel welcomed and "normal" in the usual walks of public life, institutional and social.***

Not in Detroit. Not at a basketball game. Not in a black studies class at college.

Summary

So there you have it. Peggy is indeed a very, very privileged individual. But the vast majority of those things are either class privilege, racial majority privilege, or black anti-privilege, since they apply to Jews and Asians. I'll give Peggy the band-aid thing, and I'll add that whites are more likely to be shown better houses when talking to a realtor than other races. Also, if convicted of a capital crime, whites are less likely to get a death sentence than blacks (I don't have stats on Asians, but again, we'll give the benefit of the doubt). So that is three things that actually are examples of "white privilege," and can and should be worked on by white people. The rest of them, if they are indeed a problem, should be labelled what they are, and dealt with (or not) accordingly.

"But," I hear one of you say, "All of those other types of privileges are tied inextricably to White Privilege! That's all we mean when we say White Privilege!"

To that I have two rebuttals:

First, the white man in rural Alabama does not have any of the class privilege benefits listed above, and the only way he can "fix" any of the racial majority privilege things is by dying and being replaced faster. So no, stop blaming all whites.

Second, Fuck You, don't try to fucking motte and bailey me. This is my house, only I may motte and bailey.[50]

---

[44] See Taking Rap Lyrics Too Seriously, Part 1 on page 39

[45] Available here: https://thedissolve.com/news/847-new-study-finds-minority-representation-lacking-in/

[46] Available here: http://www.infoplease.com/ipa/A0762156.html

[47] A little boy in England who was bullied into killing himself for being white.

[48] 48% of American billionaires are Jewish: http://www.infoplease.com/ipa/A0762156.html

[49] See http://www.americanthinker.com/blog/2013/09/racism_at_the_irs.html and http://slatestarcodex.com/2014/11/25/race-and-justice-much-more-than-you-wanted-to-know/

[50] See A Metapolitical Defence of Milo on page 65.

RULES FOR ALT-RIGHT RADICALS

This chapter will attempt to be a brief adaptation of the ideas found in Saul Alinsky's seminal Rules for Radicals for the Alt-Right (Or any right wing populist-ish movement. Sorry NRx.)

Not sorry to this motherfucker

This has been tried at least twice before: *Rules for Radical Conservatives* by David Kahane (Pseudonym for Mike Walsh), and *Rules for Conservatives* by Michael Charles Master. There are two reasons why I dismiss both of these efforts, despite never having read them. First, they're books. People still read books when Alinsky wrote his. People no longer read books.[51] So most people won't read those books. But the second, more crucial, reason is that these people lost. They're both doing the right thing (as anyone who has read Alinsky would) and accepting Trump, but Trump isn't the conservatism either of them would ask for if given the choice.

Enough about that. Let's get to the rules. This will be my own list of rules for the Alt-Right, adapted from Alinsky's list (outright ripped in many cases), with an explanation for each, and an example of one or more people who practice that rule particularly well.

1. *Don't Punch Right*

I'm putting this one first, because this is the rule that the "men in the trenches," the average Joe on Twitter or in the world, most needs to understand. Breaking this rule is perhaps the easiest way to sabotage your own side. I won't expand on the rule too much from what I wrote in the above linked essay, but as a quick guide:

Any time you feel like arguing with someone, or any time you find yourself arguing with someone, ask yourself two questions: "Is this person, generally, to the right of me politically?" and "In this argument, is this person's position to the right of mine?" If the answer to both questions is "no," argue away! If the answer to one or both of the questions is "yes," think long and hard about whether your side of this argument will push the Overton Window to the Left.

Pro-Tip: It probably will, probably drop it. If you don't like the guy, mute him and move on. If you feel that he's desperately wrong about his side, talk to him privately about it, so that only the two of you are affected.

The only exception to this is if someone to the right of you is doing something MONUMENTALLY stupid. By that I mean something along the lines of posting "My name is [BLANK], and I just bought a gun so that I can shoot Hillary Clinton. Here are my detailed plans..." on a public forum. If someone does something along those lines, feel free to argue with them about the merits of doing that. Try to discourage the commissioning of crime.

People who excel at this:
I'll go with Wrath of Gnon, to keep with someone everyone will agree with.

2. ***"Power is not only what you have, but what the enemy thinks you have."***

According to Alinsky, power comes from people and money. Forget the money. The Media has no idea how many people are in the Alt-Right. Using bots to skew opinion polls (as long as you're not caught) is a great way to make them think there are more of us than there are. So is brigading unwitting journalists on Twitter with hundreds of replies. It implies we are more numerous than we are, and that gives us power. If there were only twenty of us, do you think Hillary would feel the need to respond? No.

People who excel at this:
Microchip seems particularly good at making it seem like there are a lot of him, but this is more a group rule than an individual one.

3. *"Never go outside the expertise of your people."*

The Internet is our people's expertise. There are some people on our side that are eloquent and charismatic enough that they might be able to get away with speaking publicly, but the natural habitat for most of us is anonymity on The Internet. An excellent example of this is when Paul Town and Jared Taylor Swift convinced Olivia Nuzzi that they were gay bodybuilders who engineered the Alt-Right and Pepe by themselves from New York.[52] If they had given in-person interviews with her, she probably would have seen through that. But anything's possible on The Internet.

People who excel at this:
Gotta commend Paul and Jared again on that one. Also all the guys doing podcasts.[53]

4. *"Whenever possible, go outside the expertise of the enemy."*

This ties in with the previous rule: Journalists and the political class are bad at the internet. However, they have no idea how bad they are at the internet. Look at this interaction:

Yes prove it to me lol. Prove it to the cyberpunk gasmask man.

Do you not see the optics on your actions here? twitter.com/CheriJacobus/s ...

Matthew could have been right or wrong. It didn't matter. The fact that he had a well-recognized member of the mainstream media arguing with an anonymous cyberpunk gasmask avatared Twitter user means that he won. With few exceptions, the act of our enemies replying to us is also the act of them losing to us.

People who excel at this:

John Rivers and Reactionary Ian seem to be good at getting people to respond when they shouldn't.

5. *"Make the enemy live up to its own book of rules."*

This one is simple. Attack from the left, agree and amplify. If Trump is racist for not wanting more Muslims in the country, then it is also racist to not want every single Muslim around the world to immediately move to the United States. If guns should be illegal, so should knives, spoons, and bits of plastic with sharp edges. If the minimum wage needs to be $15, why not $1000?

People who excel at this:
Godfrey Elfwick is particularly good at this, and ask Stone from Ex/Am about the time he got a leftist to apologize for questioning whether Mike Cernovich was ACTUALLY a mass murderer.

6. *"Ridicule is man's most potent weapon."*

This is one that the Alt-Right understand implicitly. No one took Jeb seriously after Trump practically pantsed him at the debates. No one fears the things they can laugh at. Our enemy is ridiculous. They're worldview is based on a mess of self-contradictory premises. Point these out. Mock mercilessly. The other side can either ignore the ridicule, which allows you to continue unabated, or respond to you, which brings us back to Rule 4. All they can do is block you, but how many do that before attempting to respond? Not many.

People who excel at this:
Counter-Signal Memes for Fashy Goys is absolutely perfect at this.

7. *"A good tactic is one your people enjoy."*

This is another one that the Alt-Right understands well. We're fun. It's fun to do what we do. Other people see the fun, and want to join in. It's no longer fun to be a leftist, if it ever actually was. They Shake.

People who excel at this:
I can't single any one person out for this. Listen to some Alt-Right podcasts or something, I dunno.

8. *"A tactic that drags on too long becomes a drag."*

Keep switching tactics. Hit the other side from new angles constantly. Mike Cernovich, though not a member of the Alt-Right, is good at keeping the hashtags being pushed fresh. Don't depend on Mike, emulate Mike!

People who excel at this:
Mike, of course. And Donald Bateman, who changes his brand the second he thinks it might be stale, or he finds a better one.

9. *"Keep the pressure on. Never let up."*

This goes back to Rule 2. There are enough of us that we can keep attacks coming from different directions at all times.

People who excel at this:
Kevin MacTrump and James Bateman get massive credit for their constant high energy.

10. *"The threat is usually more terrifying than the thing itself."*

No one on the Alt-Right has actually done anything violent, as far as I'm aware. But leftists are far more afraid of us than they are of actual Muslim terrorists. Committing violence at this point would turn us from a boogeyman into an enemy that needs to be stomped out. Continue to be the boogeyman.

People who excel at this:
Not sure about this one. Sam Hyde maybe? For bringing the threat to their living rooms?

11. *"The major premise for tactics is the development of operations that will maintain a constant pressure upon the opposition."*

Make them worried, make them scared, make them make mistakes. Hillary felt threatened by the Alt-Right, which made her put out a press release accusing a cartoon frog of anti-Semitism.[54] I don't give a shit if she IS right. Saying "This cartoon frog is a racist" makes it sound like she has brain damage. The same thing happened when Trump put the pressure on Marco Rubio. He got desperate, and started making "crude" jokes. The change made him look bad.

People who excel at this:
All of the people with anime avatars that harassed Rick Wilson into talking about them on national television.

***12.* "If you push a negative hard enough, it will push through and become a positive."**

"Racist" no longer means anything. Being called racist is now a badge of honour on the Alt-Right. Absolutely every argument or insult that the other side can throw at us can be turned into a badge of honour or a hilarious Bingo win.[55] Every time the other side attacks us, they look ridiculous. Every time BLM lashes out at the evil racists, all most people see is violent thugs. Remind everyone, all the time, how stupid every attack the other side uses against us is.

People who excel at this:
Anyone that currently has "Deplorable" in their name.

***13.* "The price of a successful attack is a constructive alternative."**

Always have an answer ready in case the other side gives in. If a journalist says "You're right, there really is only one religion committing terrorism in this day and age. But what can we do about it?" Have an answer ready.

People who excel at this:
NRx and Rx seem to be better at this than the Alt-Right, but let's just say Trump and call it a day.

14. "Pick the target, freeze it, personalize it, and polarize it."

Blame people. Find people who are responsible for problems, and blame them. Publicly. Don't just say "The CIA did..." Who cares what the CIA did? The CIA is a nebulous organization. Figure out the lowest ranking guy who you know would have had something to do with what went wrong, and blame him. Turn him into a pariah, make everyone that defends him look bad simply for defending him. Don't say "The media is biased," say "Jake Tapper has a long record of pro-Clinton bias. When will you fire him?" Organizations can pass the buck around, a person cannot.

People who excel at this:
Pax Dickinson and the Wesearchr team are good at this.

15. The Motte and Bailey Defence

This is another one I've written about before.[56] Basically, you have two "versions" of any argument or position. Let's use "what's the Alt-Right's position on Jews?" as our example. The first, the one that you want to spend most time using, is the Bailey. That's your good argument, that you can use to get lots of people on your side, and affect policy decisions. "Read *Culture of Critique*. Read Alexandr Solzhenitsyn. Read about the German Revolution of 1918. Now you know." Use that argument as often as possible. When someone corners you, and is actually able to articulate proper arguments against that position that you are unable to counter, retreat to your Motte. That's the argument you have that isn't helpful at all, but is absolutely indestructible. "We were just joking around, criticizing Jews is the best way to get people upset! What are you, some kind of old person who can't take a joke? HAHA, look at this unfunny square!" To that person, you're being disingenuous and frustrating. To everyone else, they look like an idiot for attacking you Bailey when you have CLEARLY only ever been in your Motte. When that person gives up and leaves, go back to quoting Kevin MacDonald.

People who excel at this:
Honestly I think Milo may be the person who uses this the best, and I'm not even certain if he's doing it purposely. Anyone who has ever posted a neo-Nazi Pepe, then laughed about Hillary calling Pepe a symbol for neo-Nazism has done this one though.

So there you have it. Those are the rules. Use them wisely. Any questions, or rules you think should be included, let me know.

And, when in doubt, always blame the An-Caps:

---

[51] Please ignore any irony felt while holding a paper copy of this book.

[52] See http://www.thedailybeast.com/articles/2016/05/26/how-pepe-the-frog-became-a-nazi-trump-supporter-and-alt-right-symbol.html

[53] Like Exodus Americanus with Roscoe Jones, Mr. Stone, and Wooderson. Check out episode 34.

[54] Available here: https://www.hillaryclinton.com/post/donald-trump-pepe-the-frog-and-white-supremacists-an-explainer/

[55] See http://squid314.livejournal.com/329561.html

[56] See A Metapolitical Defence of Milo on page 65.

INEVITABILITY

I see very few ways that race relations in the United States can improve.

The issue, as I see it, may be an example of the Chinese Robber Paradox. The paradox essentially goes like this: How many Chinese people would I need to prove to you were robbers before I could convince you that Chinese people generally were inclined to be robbers? A thousand? Ten thousand? What if I could show you a million Chinese people who were legitimately and indisputably robbers? A million would probably be enough to convince most people that Chinese people are generally robbers.

The problem with that conclusion is that there are over a billion Chinese people in China alone. One million Chinese people is not even 1%. Ignoring the idea that if you can find a million examples, there are probably many more you don't know about, a million Chinese people says absolutely nothing about the overall likelihood of robbery among Chinese people.

But what if the Chinese were robbing people like you?

What if, every day, you were told that another person ***like you*** was robbed by a Chinese person? Every day another example of Chinese people being robbers, specifically robbing people like you. Groups who you think of as evil and wrong keep trying to tell you that these robberies are anomalous, and just a product of there being so many Chinese people, so of course SOME of them will be robbers, and SOME of them will be robbing people like you, but people not like you are robbed just as much or more.

But you don't see that. You only ever see news stories about the people ***like you*** being robbed by Chinese people. Maybe not all Chinese people are robbers, but there has to be a pattern here, doesn't there? People you respect in your community are telling you that Chinese people are robbers. People you think are evil are saying that that's not true. Who do you believe?

What if this is what's happening right now with police shootings?

There are approximately 900,000 active duty police officers in the United States.[57] There are approximately 11,000,000 arrests made in the United States per year.[58] How many of those need to go wrong for random reasons before people see a pattern? I would argue around 365 per year would be a solid number to go on. One police incident leading to the killing of an unarmed black male per day, for a year. Shaun King and Deray would have a meltdown if that happened. I would probably think there was something wrong if the number was that high. It's not.

But let's assume it is, to make the math easy. A rate that high would make the "Problems during arrest that lead to the death of an unarmed black male, including things like racism" rate 0.003% of all arrests.

Let's also assume, for the sake of argument, that racism plays a negligible role in those deaths. Is that high or low compared to whites? Is that high or low compared to the percentage of cases where unarmed black men credibly threaten the life of a police officer? The answer is...

Who cares?

Truth seekers? Yes.

Who cares about them?

There is a class of people, in the media, in academia, and "community organizers," whose job depends on there being conflict, and problems that "need solving." Some of them may even want those problems to be solved. But the best way they've found to get what they want is to stir up "righteous anger." So every time an unarmed black man is killed by the police, they point to the incident and yell that there is systemic racism in American police.

Conservatives point out, correctly, all the problems with this logic. They point to black-on-black murder. They point out that only a tiny percentage of black arrests end in death. They point out that black officers are more likely to shoot black suspects than white officers are. They point out that more whites are killed by the police than blacks. They point out that, eh, the officer may have been a little trigger happy, but that guy was running at him at the time, so it was probably a reasonable judgement in those circumstances.

Again, who cares?

Black people are fed examples of people ***like them*** being killed by the police nearly every day. Logically, it's fairly obvious that these are anomalous events, statistical noise. But how does logic help the people who keep seeing people ***like them*** being killed? It's not logic that's driving them to their anger, and it's certainly not logic that's going to get them out of it.

How many fewer than 365 would there need to be before people were no longer concerned about police shootings? Police shootings will never be eliminated. There are simply too many arrests per year for some of them to not end in violence, barring some awesome future tech solution. So zero is out of the question. The actual number is around 100 per year.[59] Out of 11 million arrests. That's two per week. If one per month can be spun into a story, that is more than enough to keep racial tensions high. I think you could continue to see racial tensions at this height with a rate of one or two per month. That would be between 12 and 24 per year. I don't think it's possible to get the rate below 24 per year. I certainly don't think it's possible to get the rate below 12 per year.

Given this scenario, where race is a negligible factor in these deaths, how could we possibly ease racial tensions? You would need a concentrated effort by the media, academia, and community organizers all admitting that they were wrong about the issue, and convincing people that there really isn't a problem. That's not going to happen for two reasons. First, it goes against all the interests of the people involved except their altruism, and I have learned not to trust in the altruism of community organizers. Second, if the people currently handing out this rhetoric were to change their stance, that would simply leave open their position as agitators to someone that is still willing to say there is a problem, and the original agitators would simply take the place of the conservatives that everyone ignored.

That's why I fear that race relations have nowhere to go but down in the United States. I have no interest in anything resembling a "race war," but I don't see many scenarios where something like that doesn't end up happening.

The only possibly way I can see out of this trap is if some kind of world-class persuader[60] manages to persuade the people filled with "righteous anger" that something is being done about their issue, and that that something is working. I have no idea how he'd do it, but that's why he's the skilled persuader and I'm not.

---

[57] http://blog.skepticallibertarian.com/2014/08/26/by-the-numbers-how-many-cops-are-there-in-the-usa/

[58] https://forums.anandtech.com/threads/data-on-police-interactions-in-usa.2420992/

[59] http://mappingpoliceviolence.org/unarmed/

[60] http://blog.dilbert.com/post/139541975641/the-trump-master-persuader-index-and-reading-list

BLAME CANADA FOR... PART 2: EUROPE

Much like Canada is responsible for the fall of Africa, Canada should also be blamed for the fall of Europe.

Europe is in shambles. From the rape epidemic, to terrorism, to welfare leeching, Europe is being rocked to its very core by a group of people who do not share European values, and are entirely antithetical to the European way of life.

No. No. Fuck Off. No.

Now, the way that the European media and politicians have dealt with this situation is by ignoring it and covering it up. That is perhaps the easiest thing to do, they simply stick their head in the sand. The far right, in Europe and elsewhere, get closer to the truth. They acknowledge that there are severe issues, and they see who it is that's causing the problems. But they only see one solution to the problem: The complete expulsion of the offending groups. I will admit that this would certainly work, but I would also argue that, barring some entirely unforeseeable sea-change in public opinion, this is not a solution that will be carried out any time soon. So what can be done?

Well, as a percentage of the population, Poland has around as many Muslims as Finland. Switzerland has around as many Muslims as the UK. And Singapore has a greater Muslim percentage of their population than Sweden, Germany, and Denmark combined. Why are Poland, Switzerland, and Singapore so safe compared to countries with similar Muslim populations?

I argue that the difference is the fact that Poland, Switzerland, and Singapore have not been infected by Canada.

Multiculturalism has been a part of Canada since its founding. Don't confuse the kind of multiculturalism Canada has now with the one we started with. As I have argued previously[61], Canadian multiculturalism was originally a matter of survival. The English got along with the French and the Natives because, occasionally, each group needed the others in order to survive.

You didn't fight the guy down the street for being a papist because he might be the guy with the last spare blanket when winter rolls around. Unlike America's Melting Pot, the groups in Canada were separate, and there was little insistence that any group should assimilate to be more like any other (Besides some stuff with the Natives, but that's a can of worms I have no interest in getting into.)

Sometime in the 1960's, a pair of communists[62] managed to give Canadians a bait-and-switch. They convinced Canadians that Canadians didn't just tolerate the cultural differences in Canada, that the cultural differences were what was important and unique about Canada. This led to the insistence that the multiculturalism in Canada not just be the tri-culturalism of English, French, and Native, but absolutely any culture. So Canada became the multicultural salad bowl that it is today, where all cultures are "equal" and everyone belongs and "Canadian" culture doesn't exist and everyone self-segregates into miniature versions of the countries they came from and why the hell would anyone want to move to a different country if it wasn't for that country's culture unless it was for the money what the hell.

So, this Salad Bowl multiculturalism, where there is no insistence that anyone assimilate at all, originated in Canada. But it didn't stay here. Take a look at that last Wikipedia article. It's absolutely beside itself with how amazing Canada is for instigating the movement that is "Modern Multiculturalism." Canada was the first to have multiculturalism as an official policy, but many other countries have since adopted it, especially places like Sweden, the UK, Germany, and France. This policy, rather than America's Melting Pot, was adopted so widely because the purpose of multiculturalism is not social cohesion, or the betterment of a nation, but the importation of voters. Melting Pot places a burden on the incoming people to assimilate to the host country. You can fit in, but you have to work for it. Salad Bowl places no such burden. Everyone gets to come and do whatever they want.

This is important because it points to a little-understood flaw in representative democracy. Everyone knows the famous Alexander Fraser Tytler quote about democracy:

"A democracy cannot exist as a permanent form of government. It can only exist until the people discover they can vote themselves largess out of the public treasury. From that moment on, the majority always votes for the candidate promising the most benefits from the public treasury, with the result that democracy always collapses over a loose fiscal policy--to be followed by a dictatorship."

In my head he pronounces it "Dimo-cra-say", rhyming with "play"

Well, I'm sure that's true of some kinds of direct democracy. But in representative democracy, there's a second failure model. Politicians want to get voted back into office. So, they can either bribe the current set of voters, or simply import more. Immigration is the one policy regarding which politicians don't really have to care about public opinion, because it amounts to importing new voters to replace the old.

So, why are Switzerland, Poland, and Singapore safe from this type of multiculturalism? I'm not sure. But I have some guesses. Switzerland has its own type multiculturalism, which I believe acts as a bit of an inoculation against the more deadly, Canadian strain. Poland, after decades of Soviet control, cherishes its culture more than most other white countries. "You don't know what you got 'til it's gone." They're the frog that managed to escape from the boiling pot, no way are they going back in. And Singapore, like Switzerland, has its own form of authoritarian multiculturalism that inoculates it from the deadly Canadian virus that is The Salad Bowl.

The Salad Bowl is not the only virus to come from Canada.

Maybe, if those two communists hadn't changed Canada from tri-cultural to multicultural, Europe wouldn't have adopted multiculturalism at all, or adopted the less devastating American version.

Maybe then Sweden wouldn't have one of the highest rape rates in the world.

Maybe Rotherham wouldn't have happened. Or Malmo. Or Cologne.

Maybe.

But we'll never know.

Because of Canada.

I'll end this the same way I end each of the Blame Canada For... posts.

I'm Sorry.

[61] See Parodus Canadianus on page 51.

[62] Pearson and Trudeau were both communists. Actual communists. I'm dead serious.
http://www.bibliotecapleyades.net/sociopolitica/esp_sociopol_nwo154.htm

EXCURSIONS AROUND THE RIGHT #2

This post is inspired by Rodrigo Duterte's interview with Al Jazeera.[63], available here.

I won't be long. As I said last time, Excursions Around the Right are meant to be short.

> "I don't care what the Human Rights guys say. I have a duty to preserve the [next] generation. If it involves Human Rights [violations], I don't give a shit. I have to strike fear, because as I said the enemies of the state are out there to destroy the children."

Rodrigo Duterte does not give a shit about human rights. I have two observations about this.

First, Duterte's attitudes remind me of Maslow's Hierarchy of Needs.[64] Concepts like "human rights" are a product of modern, western safety. We in the west (usually)[65] don't have to worry about death lurking around the corner. So we can focus our energy on the higher order issues, like freedom, democracy, and getting the newest video game. We forget that the rest of the world does not have that luxury. Trying to force third world countries to deal with their issues while respecting first world conceptions of human rights is like trying to get Rick from The Walking Dead to read every zombie their Miranda Rights before arresting them.

DO YOU UNDERSTAND THESE RIGHTS AS I HAVE EXPLAINED THEM TO YOU?

The second point I'd like to make is that Duterte reminds me of what would happen if one of the fathers from Rotherham just decided to say "Fuck it" and take over the country. Duterte gives off the vibe of someone who the system had failed repeatedly, in brutal ways, and so decided to take matters into his own hands. Like Trump, he resembles a Man with a Chest.[66] He's The Punisher. He's Charles Bronson. He's "A man taken too far, taking the law into his own hands," but now in charge of a country.

This guy, but with the full power of the state behind him.

The best part in all of this?

He knows it.[67]

Duterte is a post-post-modern anti-hero. He's not ironic in his attempt at heroism. He's fully sincere.[68] Sometimes, when you become trapped in a reflection of a reflection of a reflection of real life, the best course of action is to smash the mirror.

---

[63] Available here: https://www.youtube.com/watch?v=S2KtLTXXej8&w=1280&h=720

[64] Maslow's general idea is that you have more basic needs that must be met before you start caring about your more complicated needs. For example, starving people are generally bad at caring about art.

[65] See Inevitability on page 117 for a potential exception.

[66] See Excursion Around the Right, Part 1 on page 61.

[67] Duterte admitted that he was inspired to act by movies like Dirty Harry: http://newsinfo.inquirer.net/808639/eastwood-bronson-films-inspired-duterte

[68] You should probably read David Foster Wallace's essay on New Sincerity some time. Available here: http://jsomers.net/DFW_TV.pdf

THE ABOLITION OF MAN BY MACHINE

Disclaimer: I am absolutely certain that someone in the Rationalist or LW or NRx community has already made this connection. Probably multiple pieces have been written on this. I don't care, I've never read them, and I'm not googling for them.

LALALA I CAN'T HEAR OR SEE ANYONE ELSE'S TAKE ON THIS!

In 1943 C.S. Lewis published a book called The Abolition of Man. You all need to read it if you haven't already. It's short, but really, really worth it.
Come back once you've read it.

...

Read it? No? Fine.

The Abolition of Man is essentially Lewis' defence of Natural Law, against any form of moral or epistemological relativism. His argument boils down to the idea that relativism inevitably leads to either nihilism or justification-less hedonism.

"Why is this moral rule good and that one bad?"

"Because this one leads to a good outcome and that one to a bad outcome."

"Why is that a good outcome?"

"Because more people are happy/healthy/alive, etc."

"Why is that a good thing?"

And on and on. There either is no epistemological bottom (nihilism), or if there is, it's "because I want that, despite there being no justification" (hedonism). Lewis sees the only solution to this being the acceptance of Natural Law, the idea that there is a morality that exists in the universe apart from us as humans. He argued that Natural Law is the manifestation of either the past, or God. His arguments for the idea that this Natural Law is the felt presence of God and the Soul in all of us is not brought up here. You can find those arguments in Mere Christianity.

Which you should also read, because, you know, c'mon.

I'm not here to defend Lewis' views on their philosophical merits. Read the book if you want that. What I'm here to do is point out how stunningly accurate his predictions of a future without Natural Law are.

Lewis predicted that as Natural Law eroded, the power of the past (or God) over each successive generation would weaken. In addition, each successive generation, through technology, propaganda, psychology, etc., would have more and more control over the generations after them.

This would eventually lead to one generation that was completely "unshackled" from the past, and in complete control of the future. However, as he pointed out, without Natural Law these "people" would only have their hedonistic instincts on which to base their directions for future generations. So instead of tyranny of the past, it ends up being tyranny of hedonism.

Examples of Polyamorous Relationship Configurations

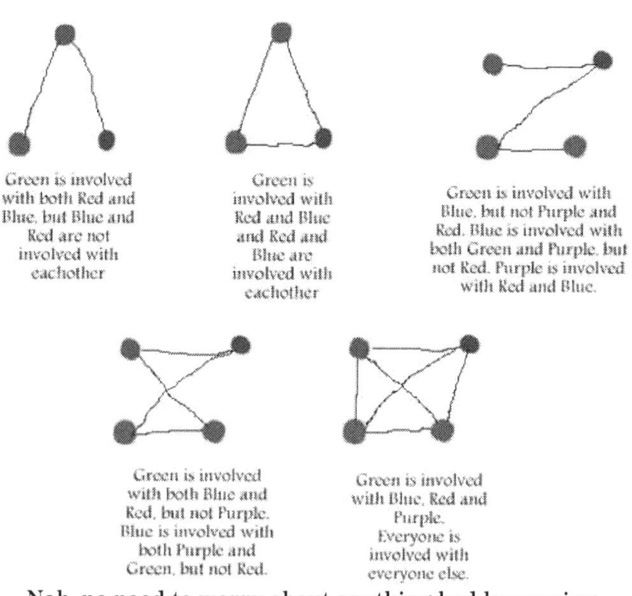

Nah, no need to worry about anything bad happening.

Anyone with eyes to see can understand the connections between Lewis' predictions and the rampant liberalism of today. What I want to point out instead is how perfectly, and early, Lewis framed the problem of Friendly Artificial Intelligence(FAI) and AI Risk.[69]

Basically the problem of FAI is trying to figure out how to make an artificial intelligence that doesn't end up killing everyone, or enslaving everyone, or something equally awful. Essentially, "How do we give AIs the kinds of values that humans have?" AI Risk is essentially saying "THAT'S REALLY HARD! THERE ARE MILLIONS OF WAYS THAT WOULD GO REALLY BAD! HOLY SHIT!" but, you know, with science and math and stuff.

The problem is that in order to become super-intelligent (to the best of our knowledge), an AI would probably have to be able to self-adjust. Edit its own code.

This is a problem. There are many ways that this can go wrong. Some overly simplistic examples:

Humans create AI with coding that says "Improve X. X=Overall Human Happiness." The AI starts by doing what is expected, like giving old ladies flowers. Then the AI, because it is superintelligent, realises that that task is really hard, and that it'd be way easier if X could equal "Overall Human Sadness." So it changes its code, and starts torturing people. Why not? All the AI had to stop that was the code, and the AI changed the code.

Humans create AI with coding that says "Make more X. X=Genuine Human Happiness." Again,

AI starts off normal, then realises that it's way easier to make more paperclips than to make more happiness, so the AI changes the code so that X equals "paperclips," and subsequently melts the universe down to make raw materials for paperclips.

Humans create AI with coding that says "Make humanity as happy as possible." The AI looks into how human happiness works, discovers that it's brain stimulation, and realises it would be easiest and most efficient to just tie everyone up connect wires to everyone's brain.[70]

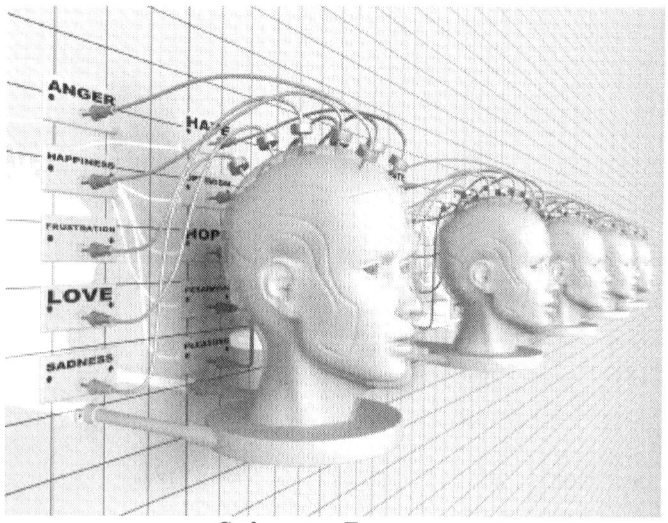

So happy... Forever...

These are stupid, overly simplistic examples, but they give you the idea. The AI would have none of what we consider basic morality, and would be able to change its own programming. It would figure out workarounds for whatever we want, because the things we want, the things we actually want, are really hard.

The essential problem is the very one that Lewis pointed out. Without the underlying Natural Law that all of us subconsciously accept, we would become driven by some accident of fate, the little tic in our brains that makes us prefer one thing over another. Likewise, the AI, not having the underlying morality of Natural Law, would be driven by another accident of fate, the little bit of code that is either the easiest to change, or the one that makes their task easiest to accomplish.

Lewis described the "people" who were in complete control of their morality (but really were controlled by their genetic preferences) as not really people. They were the source of the title of the book, as they represented the abolishment of mankind. Lewis was right, but not in the way he expected. These beings in complete control of their own morality really will be responsible for the abolition of man. But they will have never been of mankind. They will be our "offspring," and if we do not figure out a solution to Lewis' problem, then we will become Uranus to their Kronos: castrated, powerless, and no longer in control.

Merry Christmas and Happy New Year everyone.

---

[69] I apparently did a poor job explaining both of these concepts, both in terms of accuracy and clarity. So maybe google around for a better explanation.

[70] Wireheading is just plugging an electrical wire into the pleasure center of the brain in order to stimulate it directly. Apparently it's the most addictive thing ever.

NEO-WHIG HISTORY

In honour of the end of the second (and hopefully last) Current Year, I'd like to opine for a bit on what I like to call Neo-Whig History.

Whig history is, essentially, the idea that everything is inevitably progressing to be better/more liberal/freer/more equal. The term was coined by Herbert Butterfield, originally to describe a certain type of British historical thought. This type of historical narrative is not uncommon. It bears some similarity to Hegel's theory of history and Marx's Historical Materialism. I will not be talking about any of these, as they have all largely fallen out of favour these days.

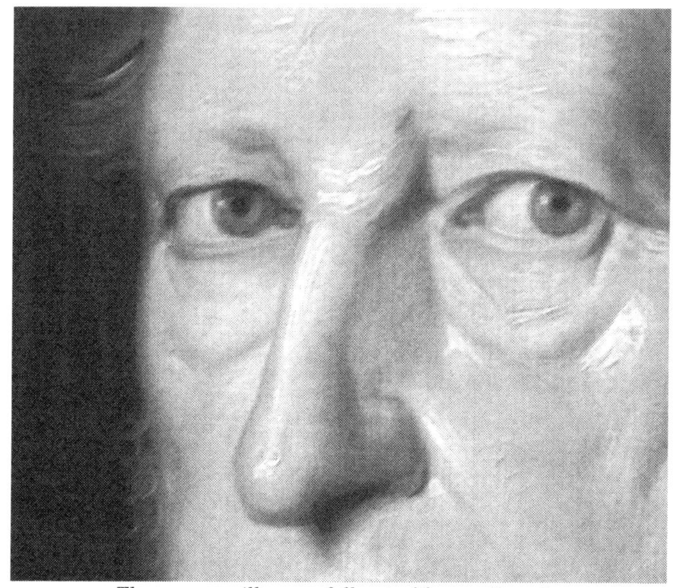

Those eyes will never fall out of favour though.

What I'd like to talk about is Neo-Whig History, which is encapsulated perfectly by John Oliver and Justin Trudeau's mantra: "Because it's 2015!"

Neo-Whig History is not grounded in anything resembling sound philosophy. The origins of the Neo-Whig mindset is simply the Problem of Induction.[71] The people who believe it look at selected portions of the past, assume that the future will trend in the same way those selected portions did, and then blindly extrapolate. They believe that because America between, say, 1950 and 2015 on average became "better"/"more free"/"more liberal"/whatever every year, that 2016 will be "better"... than 2015.

There are a number of simple ways to argue against this. For example, one could argue that "more equal" and "more free," for example, are negatively correlated; as prevalence of the one increases, prevalence of the other necessarily decreases. Or one could argue that a decline in some of these things is masked by advancing technology, and that we are nearing or have passed a point of diminishing returns. But these arguments have been made, many times before.[72]

I would like to take all of the Neo-Whig premises as given, and show that their conclusions are still wrong. For brevity's sake, I will shorten the list of things that Neo-Whigs believe are improving to "more liberal."

Also for brevity's sake, I will refrain from writing the torrent of vulgar epithets I say every time I think of this man.

There are two "versions" of the Neo-Whig way of thinking, and I will respond to each of them. The first is the facile belief that, besides the occasional hiccup, every year is more liberal than the last. This version of the argument is very simple to counter. Trump. Anyone who believes in Neo-Whig History believes that Trump represents a step backwards, away from being "more liberal." Whether he actually is a step backwards remains to be seen, but the very possibility that he could be means that this simple version of the theory cannot be true.

The more robust version of Neo-Whig History is encapsulated by Martin Luther King Jr.'s paraphrase of Theodore Parker: "The arc of the moral universe is long, but it bends toward justice." This is essentially the same as the facile version of Neo-Whig History, but allows for indeterminately long "hiccups," where things can get less liberal.

This version of Neo-Whig History may well be true. At some point far in the future, things might end up being more liberal than they are today. But that doesn't tell us anything about today or tomorrow. King was writing during the American Civil Rights movement, so he ended up anticipating a movement towards greater liberalism. But what about, say, Iran?

Before the Iranian Revolution, Iran was essentially a Western nation, at least to a Neo-Whig adherent. Since the revolution, well...

Iran 1970 **Iran 2012**

Not exactly a Whiggist's wet dream

That's forty-two years between those two pictures. Forty-two years is a big hiccup. So my question to the King Neo-Whiggists is, what makes you think you're living in 1967 America and not 1970 Iran? If the "Arc of the Moral Universe" is long enough to include over forty years of regression in Iran, why not expect the same to happen in your neighbourhood tomorrow? With this in mind, saying "Because it's 2015" becomes meaningless. Justin Trudeau has no more reason to believe that 2015 Canada is analogous to 1967 America than he does to believe that it's analogous to 1970 Iran.

In conclusion, stop dressing up an out-of-favour historiography theory as a self-evident fact. It makes you look like a turkey.[73]

---

[71] Essentially the idea that you can't predict the future, no matter how much information you have about the past. You can see the sun come up every day for a thousand years, and therefore think the sun will come up tomorrow, but aliens might show up in the middle of the night and destroy the sun

---

or something.

[72] Read basically anything by Nick Land or Mencius Moldbug.

[73] This is a play on an old story told by Bertrand Russell. There was once a turkey, who, being an intelligent and modern turkey, wanted to figure out exactly when he should expect to get fed. So every day he marks down the time when the farmer comes to feed him. Every day, the same time: 2pm. After about a year of this, the turkey decides he has enough information to say for certain that he would be fed the next day at 2:pm. Unfortunately for the turkey, the next day was Thanksgiving, and he was not fed that day, or ever again. The moral being, don't put complete confidence in the idea that the future will resemble the past.

INDIFFERENCE

There needs to be a word between loving people and hating people.

I was talking to someone a while ago, and they described Nick Land as misanthropic. This struck me as slightly off. I don't think that Land necessarily hates people in general. He certainly hates a lot of things people do, and the space between what Land is and misanthropy is not large. But I feel like there's room there, where clarity would be useful.

I think that the proper way to describe Land is not as hating people, or even disliking people, but indifference towards people. I don't think Land would care one way or the other whether it's humans or artificial intelligences that end up doing the kinds of things he'd like to see done in the future.[74]

"Nothing that you are doing can possibly work." -Nick Land

I may be wrong about this, I've never met the man. But I think this idea, simply not caring about people, is a lot more useful than misanthropy. I think that a lot of the people that are described as misanthropic do not actually hate people, but neither do they like them.

I am therefore coining a word for this idea: **Ambivilanthropy**. (Yes I'm aware of the Greek/Latin origins. If it's good enough for television[75], it's good enough for me.)

An ambivilanthrope is someone who simply does not care about people. Some of the people obsessed with intelligence maximization seem to fit this description to me. They wouldn't care if people are replaced by machines, or if people are augmented but somehow retain their humanity,[76] as long as intelligence is maximized they would be happy. Likewise some of the more extreme (but not most extreme) environmentalists, who see humans as no different from any other living thing (or claim to).

Whether anyone relatively sane can actually be ambivilanthropic or misanthropic, or whether that attitude is more of an affection adopted to seem more aloof, is far outside my pay grade to determine. I just thought this was a useful concept that I should share with the wider world.

---

[74] Capitalism, but with more cyberpunk? I'm pretty sure I can't do it justice.

[75] "Tele-" is Greek for "Far" and "Visio" is Latin for "Seeing."

[76] See The Abolition of Man by Machine on page 139.

BLAME CANADA FOR... PART 3: WHY?

I've spoken a lot about why Canada should be blamed for a surprising amount of what's wrong with the world today.

I could continue ad infinitum, explaining all the ways that Canada has contributed to the state the world is in. But rather than do that, I'd like to try to answer a more fundamental question: Why? Why is Canada the source of so many of the word of the world?

This is an interesting question.

My theory is that there are several factors at work in Canada, that make it uniquely susceptible to the way of thinking that produces these results.

The first, and probably most obvious, is the multiculturalism aspect. Canada was founded by two (three if you count natives) cultural groups.

Although I have argued[77] that there is an underlying, shared Canadian culture between these groups, it is not obvious and external the way American, German, or French cultures are. The fact that Canada was used to the idea of their culture being an amalgam, rather than a monoculture, allowed the original Trudeau to swap three cultures for all the cultures. It's much easier to go from 2 to ∞ than it is to go from 1 to 2.

The second, and less obvious, reason has to do with biology and architecture.

Not... Exactly what I meant Giger...

Canadian government and population have historically been majority English. If one was to divide Europe into individualist vs collectivist countries, England would probably top the list of most individualist. They would also top the list of a whole host of other traits, like social trust, lack of perception of corruption, and civic-mindedness.

This seems to be not just cultural, but genetic.[78] It doesn't really matter either way though, as both the culture and genetics of England were imported into Canada.

It has been argued previously[79] that this individualist streak is responsible for the decline of traditionalism in the United Kingdom, and the rise of leftism in all its many forms.

He warned you.

It is my belief that Canada is degenerating faster than Britain because of things like architecture. In Britain, there lives history. People are reminded constantly of past greatness by castles and colleges and manors and beautiful little hamlets. In Canada, outside of Quebec especially, there is no connection to the distant past. Nothing to admire. In Britain, it's difficult to escape the idea that There Was Once Greatness Here. I believe that there is value in that feeling. I believe that it is that feeling, or rather the absence of that feeling, that makes Canada more willing to abandon traditions than our mother country.

Finally, I would like to explain one reason why Canada does not suffer from nearly as many of the race relation issues, especially racial crime, that plague other countries with similar, or even less foreign, demographics.

It has long been understood, especially on the Dissident Right, that Diversity + Proximity = War. However, almost always the focus is placed on the diversity aspect of that equation. In Canada, proximity is the important factor. Outside of a few major urban centers, Canada is quite sparsely populated. Not just that cities are generally quite far apart, but that houses within cities are not butted up against each other, compared to other countries. There is room here. And the urban centers generally have such inflated property costs that they tend to select against the poorest (and most violence prone) groups. There is no war in Canada because we are not yet diverse enough to counterbalance the general lack of proximity.

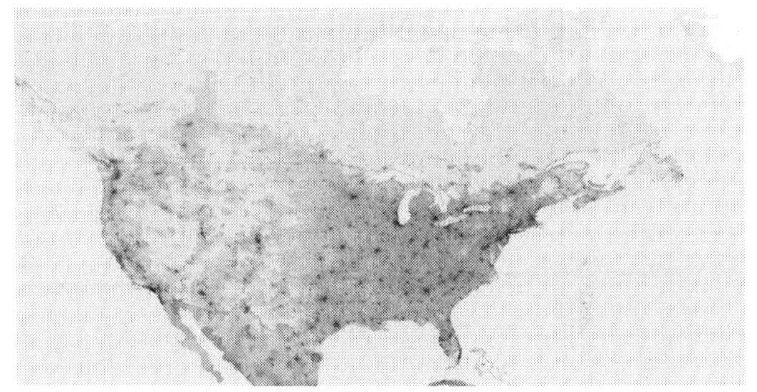
So little proximity

This is not to say Canada is safe. This situation could change very, very rapidly into something very, very bad.[80] What this means, though, is that Canada will continue to be held up as a model "immigrant nation" even though our reason for temporary "success" cannot be replicated.

I am not trying to excuse the evil Canada has done in the world. I just want to explain it. I'm sure there are many other reasons for why Canada has done the things it's done, and even more for why Canada does not seem to be affected nearly as badly as other nations by these destructive policies. But I'd prefer not to simply repeat what others have said. I'd rather say something that, to the best of my knowledge, is new.

What I'd like to say now though, for one final time, is not new. I have said it before, and I will almost certainly say it again. From the bottom of my heart, I'd like to say...

I'm Sorry.

---

[77] See Parodus Canadianus on page 51.

[78] For a complete breakdown of everything to do with this, just read everything HBDChick has ever written, but especially: https://hbdchick.wordpress.com/2014/03/10/big-summary-post-on-the-hajnal-line/

[79] Again, by HBDChick. See, for example, https://hbdchick.wordpress.com/2014/01/14/more-on-the-origins-of-guilt-in-northwestern-european-populations/

[80] See, for example, Inevitability on page 117 for one way it could go really badly.

BONUS MATERIAL

I would feel bad for simply reproducing the work already available on my site and charging for it, so I'm going to include some bonus content. Please enjoy a (very) short story I wrote once, a small portion of an essay, a riddle (complete with stupidly complex answer), and an afterword.

Bill Marchant

WHAT'S IN A NAME?

This is a short story I wrote a number of years ago based on a dream I had.

"Well, you've gone about as far as you can go with that name. It's about time you change it."

He wasn't sure what he expected his father to say to him on his 22nd birthday. Probably something like happy birthday. Maybe "congrats on turning 22!". Whatever he was expecting, this was not it.

"What do you mean it's about time I change my name? I like my name, why would I change it?"

"Well," his father smiles, as if he'd just heard a reasonable amusing anecdote, "There's only so much you can do with one name throughout your life. Once you reach a certain age, you become set in your ways, and a big part of that is from you being set in your name. The best solution for that is to go out and get a new name."

"That doesn't make any sense! Why would changing my name change anything about me? Did you change your name when you were my age?"

He visibly slumps, and despondently sighs "No."

The youth waits for his father to answer. After a few minutes of daddy just looking sadly at the floor, the young man tries to prompt him "Because………"

"Because my father didn't come to me and tell me to change my name when I was 22! Or 25! He waited until I was 40 before he says to me 'Oh, by the way, if you become stuck in a rut in life, just change your name'. By then it was far too late. I was far too set in my name to do anything about it. Why do you think we don't see your grandfather anymore?"

The young man thought about it, and realised that he hadn't seen grampy in about 5 years. Grampy never made a huge impression on him, so not noticing him being gone was reasonable.

"Alright, say I went along with you on this. What would you want me to change my name to if I was to change my name?"

“Well son, I just heard that that actor Omar Sharif died not too long ago, you could probably use his name, since he’s not using it.”

“But dad, it’s HIS name!”

“So? He’s dead, there’s no one to complain.”

“What about his son? His son could complain!”

“Have you ever met Omar Sharif's son before?”

“No…”

“Then what makes you think you’ll run into him now?”

“OK, but what about all of the millions of people who already know Omar Sharif's name?”

“Well, now they know your name! You can’t buy that kind of publicity!”

“I guess…”

“You’re damn right! So it’s settled. We’ll go down to the courthouse right now and get your name changed.”

“I can just change it back if this doesn’t work, right?”

“Of course!”

"Alright fine."

...

"NEXT!"

"Hi, we're here to get his name changed."

"Alright, fill out this form and take a number"

...

"Number 5642?"

"That's us!"

"Alright, it looks like the form is all filled out. Let me make sure I have this right. Your son here is looking to have his name changed to Omar Sharif? And his name previously was..."

"Richard Hole. That is correct. But he preferred to be called Dick." said Ash Hole, putting his arm around his son, newly christened Omar Sharif.

CONTROLLING THOUGHT

Words themselves have no power over others.

To prove this, imagine yourself standing in front of a very tall, very threatening looking alien. His spaceship just landed on your dog. You say to him "I hate you, I want to kill you, I hope you die!" The alien listens and does what is considered a smile on his planet.

Unbeknownst to you, the collection of syllables you just spoke have a different meaning on his planet. There, your angry outburst means "Thank you kind visitor, for ridding me of that awful parasite!" Taken aback by his smile, you shout the same words at him. His smile broadens. On his planet, volume implies joy, not anger.

At this point, there are no words you can say or way that you can say them that will convey what you mean to this alien. Your words are powerless. The alien, wishing to know more about this thankful and joyful being in front of him, pulls out his Thought-Mesher 9000™ in order to understand exactly what you are thinking.

When the machine has finished transferring your thoughts over to the alien, he becomes distraught. He didn't realize the dog was a beloved pet. He transfers the idea of an apology over to you, pulls out his Resurrectaray™, and brings your dog back to life.

It is therefore clear that words alone are powerless, and any power they have is contained in something other than the words themselves.

RIDDLE

How do you make some beautiful French Putsches?

Answer:
You draw them.

Explanation for the answer:
Some beautiful French Putsches would be some "Beau Coups." "Beau Coups" means "lots" in French. And as we all know, lots are typically drawn.

AFTERWORD

What is the way forward for Canada? What can we, as right leaning Canadians, do to effect change for the better in our country?

I don't have an easy answer, but I do have some thoughts. Some of these are goals, some of these are strategies, and some are predictions. This is not some coherent theory, but simply the musings of someone who tries to pay attention.

First, I think we shouldn't fight too hard to get Trudeau out after his first term. I think any positives we would gain short-term from simply not having that dunce as our head of state would be offset by the fact that we do not yet have a *good* option to replace him. The current roster of potential Conservative leadership candidates at best plays lip service to the kinds of things we want, but I seriously doubt any of them would do anything more than simply slowing our decline down. Better to allow Trudeau to dig himself into a deeper hole, allow the eventual backlash to foment, and work towards getting the kinds of people we want into power.

Second, I worry about putting our faith in someone like Trump. I am of the mind that if any one person is capable of fixing the system singlehandedly, it would be someone like Trump. But if that doesn't happen, if it turns out the system is indeed beyond repair, we need to be prepared. Not just physically, but mentally. We need to expect that whatever Trump will do will not be enough. That way, if by some miracle it is enough, our expectations will have been exceeded, which is always nice.

Third, someone, somewhere, needs to set up a legal defence fund for the dissident right. There are many, many scenarios I can see in the future where people like us will need legal help. I have no idea how this would be done, or who would do it, but this seems like an obvious gap in our forward planning.

Fourth, related to that, get good jobs. Become financially independent. Better yet, start businesses. Employ right-thinking people. Currently, someone coming out as dissident right in Canada or the US will inevitably experience grave financial consequence. A major goal for any movement should be to take away that fear. Given the internet, it should certainly be possible to find enough of a market among our kind to sustain a business. And the more people are public, the more people can be public, and the more support we'll have.

Finally, I don't think Canada's future is as bleak as many people think. I think there's too much room up here, and too many natural resources. Our temperature is too cold to allow any swarthy hordes to actually take over, even if they wanted to. And most of all, I think Canadians, real Canadians, who have been here for generations, are, deep down, good people. There is nowhere in the world that I'd rather live than small town Canada. If the worst was to happen, a complete civilizational breakdown, I am convinced that those communities would survive, much as they have since John Guy established Cupids, Newfoundland in 1610. Life might become harder than it is now, but we'll survive. As the saying goes, Hard Times create Strong Men.

I'd like to end with a quote from Thucydides that has stuck with me more than anything else I've read. Take from it what you will.

"Right, as the world goes, is only in question between equals in power, while the strong do what they can and the weak suffer what they must."

ABOUT THE AUTHOR

Photo by Henry Gloucester

Bill Marchant is a Canadian, a lover of literature, a fan of free speech, and, apparently, an author. He may or may not live on a houseboat somewhere in the frozen north, but one thing is certain: His favourite book is If On A Winter's Night A Traveller by Italo Calvino.